BREAKING
BLACK
BARRIERS

ANDREW   BOARD

EYE GIFT PUBLISHING
4266 E. Ponce De Leon Ave.
Clarkston, GA, 30021

Introduction:

I see it all too often…

The hard looks when we make eye contact. The judgement of what I have instead of who I am. The statistics that always make us look bad. The battle between generations, the gender wars, the diaspora wars. The disconnect between African Americans Blacks from all over the world.

I feel it all too often…

Assuming the worst of me. The negative reactions to everything I do. The lack of trying to relate to me. Talking to me from a place of condemnation instead of love. The talking down on me instead of having a discussion.

I hear it all too often…

"You sound white."

"Dark skinned women are less attractive."

"Our men are pathetic."

"This generation is horrible."

"Black owned businesses are so unprofessional."

"Well, you know it won't work because Black people will find a way to mess it up."

"You not Black."

Ok just stop. I've heard enough and I'm tired of hearing it. Now it's time for me to do something about it.

About the Author:

I was born in Marietta GA, but I was raised in Cleveland, Ohio. I don't have any fancy degrees or a title like "Doctor." I do have an abundance of real-life experiences that have helped me write this book.

While in Cleveland, OH, I lived in the hood and in the suburbs. During my elementary school years, I attended schools that were balanced in having just as many White students as Black students. By my high school years, I would go to a predominantly Black high school, Collinwood High School. It was a great school but no doubt it was a hood environment. Rival gangs attended this school, and its location was in a neighborhood that had all the settings of being in the hood.

During my college years I attended Walsh University which was a predominately White institution. After 3 years of attending this school, I would transfer to Notre Dame College, which had significantly more Black students but was a predominately White institution, nonetheless. I know the awkwardness and the racial undertones that can come with being one of the few Black students on campus. It wasn't all bad however, as such an environment fostered a fraternal unity among the few Black students on campus.

I know what its like to operate in an all-Black environment, but I also know what its like to be the only Black person in a classroom. I worked at Black and White owned businesses alike and I understand the pros and cons to both entities. I know the social dynamics of the expectations others have for me because of my race.

When I was in college, I worked in a nursing home with senior citizens and I worked as a Community Mentor providing services for at-risk youth whom of which were mostly Black. I saw what the lack of guidance and resources can do to young people. I know from a firsthand standpoint the issues they face. The elders told me during my time with them the issues they've had in the past and the concerns they have for the current generations and the future.

In 2014 I would move to Atlanta, GA, where I would work in an environment once more where I was the minority. My experience in such an environment gave me some reference as to what other Black people may experience in similar settings. Eventually I would become a full-time entrepreneur starting off as a tattoo artist.

After a few years in the industry, I opened a tattoo shop with a business partner for 3 years. I know the obstacles a Black person would face opening and managing a business. At the tattoo shop, I would establish bonds with clients of all ages and backgrounds. Most of my clients are young Black men and women. Tattoo appointments are long which allowed conversations with these clients.

As I talk to them and get to know them, I often find myself impressed with their thoughts, actions, and ideas. I also gained wisdom of their issues and concerns from these conversations. I would also work as an after-school art teacher for 2 years and I would be honored to speak at Career Day for elementary school students from the last couple of years. Theirs many young people that get overlooked because of the perception of young Black people. My hope and belief in the youth is strengthen by my time and conversations with them.

Along with being a tattoo artist I also started an arts entertainment business called **Strokes Mobile Sip & Paint**. As an Arts Instructor the majority of my clients are women spanning from young, middle aged, to elderly. During these parties many conversations come up about their thoughts, and ideas of the world around them. I get to hear their thoughts and concerns during their sip & paint parties.

I know what it's like to experience racism from other races, but I also know what it's like to receive great things from non-Black people. I know what its like to be accepted and rejected by my own people. I know what it's like to be called "White" for speaking too well, but I also know what its like to be thought of as a thug because of my skin tone. I've been in environments where my Blackness was seen as a gift and in others a curse.

I have an abundance of experiences, conversations, and face to face interactions with Black people on a full spectrum. I know what its like to be in a variety of settings that were welcoming and hostile. I've been part of the minority and the majority, and I understand the feelings that come with both settings. I also know and understand the potential of Black people to be even greater than what they are.

When we pass off from this life, you should be able to look back at one's actions and let it define who they were and what they stood for. We should all aim to leave something behind in this lifetime that can benefit others long after we are gone. This is one of the many solutions I'm offering my people of my time and beyond:
Breaking Black Barriers.

"Few burdens are heavy when everybody lifts"
-Charles Evers.

"We will achieve greatness together or failure apart."
-Hazel Johnson.

"We'd better pull together before the forces pull us apart."
-Willie Brown.

Systematic oppression along with negative stereotypes have made some Black people devalue themselves as individuals and as a community. As Black people try to make sense of this time of oppression that we are trying to live and prosper in one question remains, how can we accomplish anything divided?

How can we build strong institutions and progress towards a better future when we don't like, value, and believe in one another? How can we see ourselves accomplishing anything if we don't know our history or have knowledge of self?

No matter what we want to do as Black people we are better off doing it together and united than alone. The negative stereotypes associated with Black men and women have been so broadly accepted on a global scale that even Black people themselves tend to buy into and believe these negative stereotypes as a fact when dealing with each other.

Some of these popular negative stereotypes are: being classless, "ghetto", poor, naive, bad with money, bad with credit, not self-sufficient, I could go on. The only "positive" stereotypes regarding

Blacks people is being athletic, great musicians, and setting the trend for what's "cool" and trendy in pop culture. Some of these positive stereotypes have reaped benefits for Black people but for the few not the majority.

The purpose of this book is to unite Black people and for us to see value in ourselves so we can build towards a better future together. Yes, systematic and global racism has been detrimental to the growth of Black people however, it will be harder to take on these issues divided, and we will be better off fighting these issues untied.

One may ask "How can Black people become more united?" We have to see value in ourselves, value in each other, seek knowledge of Black history, build Black businesses, build Black institutions, build platforms that we own, and lastly the community has to believe and support one another. No matter how much we would want to fight those who oppress us we will never be able to overcome anything when we are going against each other.

You will find yourself fighting with more confidence in a foxhole with other soldiers than taking on the battles Black people face every day by yourself. This author believes in the future prosperity of Black people, however now even in 2023 I hate how we treat each other sometimes. If we think negatively about each other, we won't network together. And if we don't network with each other we will fail to build economic and beneficial institutions needed for a strong community.

Contents:

Acknowledgments:

This book is dedicated to the original people in which all people around the globe originate from. To the ancient kings and queens in African societies whom stories remain hidden from history and are not accounted for in the history books of formal education. To Black civilizations that were some of the greatest societies in human history. To the ancient Black ancestor that traveled to the Americas well before Christopher Columbus.

To the African societies that fought off European imperialism. To the aboriginal Australian's who fought for the right to exist. To the forgotten Black kingdoms in ancient China. To the slaves who had to cross the Atlantic in bondage. To the slaves in Haiti who revolted and were a part of the most successful slave rebellion in world history against the French. To the slaves who had to endure some of the worst treatment in human history in the Americas and Caribbeans. To the slaves who risked their lives to run away from the plantations and fought for others slaves to be free. To the first person to die for American freedom. To the Black soldiers who fought for their for their freedom during the American Civil War.

To those who had to learn to read and write a language that was foreign to them at a rate in which no other race has since. To those who had to survive as third class citizens during the Reconstruction period all the way until the Civil Rights Movement. To the Black ancestors who still manage to hold down jobs and start businesses as third class citizens. To the excellence that was Black Wall Street which was destroyed out of nothing but pure jealousy.

To the Buffalo soldiers who were some of the fiercest fighters of that time, to the veterans of World War I and World War II who fought with pride and valor yet would not be recognized until decades later. To the Korean War and Vietnam veterans who fought for a country that would not fight for them. To the Civil Rights Movement and the Black Panthers who risked their lives and careers to demand the fair treatment and societal equality for Black people. To the Black entertainers and inventors who still went on to achieve greatness in the face of racism.

To the Black trend setters who gave America and the world its best forms of entertainment. To the survivors of Jim Crow, Mass Incarceration, the War on Drugs, and the Crack Epidemic. To my great relatives who had to endure racism and bigotry on the job just to provide for their family.

To my parents and my uncles and aunts who had to fight every day just because they went to a predominantly White high school. To my family and parents who survived and still made a way while dealing with oppression and racism in their adult years. To my mother and my father who came together, found love, and raised a family in a world that can be cruel towards Black people. To my bother and sister who managed to be successful in a better world but a racist one nonetheless. And to upcoming generations in which it is our job to make sure they live in a better world than the one we endured. I appreciate you all more than you know.

To my mother, I thank you for everything! To my aunt, thanks for always being there. Thanks to my Dad for everything he provided for me. Thanks to all my family members that share good times with me. A thank you to the ancestors before me who paved the way, and a thank you to the younger generation who will carry us into the future. And, lastly a thanks to you for reading!

Who This Book Is For

Given the title of this book, of course this book is for the betterment of the full spectrum of Black people. The text in the passages ahead are meant to bring Black people together to rely on each other, grow together, and love each other. In this authors opinion theirs many people of color who understand the importance of togetherness but, theirs also a large population of Black people who despise their own race and believe the community itself will accomplish very little than what they already has.

This book is meant to speak to both people; the ones who are optimistic and those who are pessimistic about our future. If any of the concepts in this book speak to you, I hope it can change you for the better. If you have a strong sense of self love, my hope is that this book reinforces the love you have for yourself but also for others that look like you.

Should non-Black people read this book? Of course they can and should! For non-Black people of color who face similar oppression, the same concepts can be adopted for you and your people. Should a White person read this book? Yes! Theirs some White people who work in professions where they interact with Black people on a daily basis or spend the majority of their time around Black people. Some of these people include teachers, coaches, and social workers, (just to name a few) where the majority of the people you may do your job for are Black.

This could be a reference for team building among the group you are in charge of, or you may refer this book for students, team, or clients to read. If you are going to spend the majority of your time around Black people it would be a good idea to understand Black culture and the issues they face that you may not be aware of.

Most of all this book is for those who want to see Black people do well, be healthy, happy, and succeed. When strong Black people who have love for themselves and love for each other come together great things can happen.

WE WILL KNOW
OUR HISTORY

In order for Black people to value each other we first must value ourselves. The problem is that from my view point a large majority of people only gain knowledge of history from what they learn in school and possibly what they hear from other people. Some Black people may not see themselves as valuable because their only knowledge of Black history is of slavery and oppression. The book ***Black Fatherhood The Guide To Male Parenting***, recalls the words of the great Marcus Garvey:

" A people without a past is like a tree without roots. Every black leader before and after Garvey has paid homage to Africa. They understand that the black experience did not begin with slavery. For their were African kingdoms, empires, political, social, and economic systems centuries before the existence of America."

Many Black people globally are educated on Black/African history before slavery but not nearly enough. Of course theirs an abundance of instances of overcoming obstacles and progress that Black people should be proud of. Whether its stories of Harriet Tubman or Frederick Douglass who escaped slavery all just to turn around and fight against the very forces that oppressed them through way of the underground railroad and being a abolitionist public figure, to Malcolm X and Martin Luther King who put their lives on the line during the Civil Rights era in the 1960's to the fight for self sufficiency and self community with Angela Davis and Huey P. Newton. Black people have plenty to be proud of in spite of oppressive ideologies the collective has had to endure like slavery, the Jim Crow era, "The War On

Drugs", red lining, the wealth gap, housing discrimination, and mass incarceration.

These commonly known facts about Black history share our oppression, resistance, and triumph. Most of what Black children/teens will learn in schools about Black history will be from the account of the horrors of our oppression and our resistance of those forces. A lot of these narratives will be horror stories, strife, and pain in our existence. Some will think that the oppression facing Black people is so great, that the community is doomed to the fate of what others are willing to give and not what they can have for themselves.

I believe this has a varying affect on Black people depending on how their mindset is. For some it will make them have a sense of pride and an urge to do better for the community as a whole, and for others it may make them see Black people as less valuable or weak minded. This is why its imperative for Black people to know their history before slavery. So they can hear the narrative of Black kings, queens, and prosperous societies. This way they can understand the narrative of Black royalty and not just Black oppression.

In The Mali Empire (1226-1670 Africa) ruled by Mansa Musa from 1312 to 1337 had cities like Timbuktu which was at the time one of the richest regions of the world. It is said the Mansa Musa is estimated to be the richest man to ever live having today's equivalent to 400 billion dollars and more in resources. Timbuktu became a city of education, universities, mosques, and libraries. Take the top 5 billionaires in now 2023 and add them all up and it still will not equal up to the fortune Mansa Musa assembled in his lifetime.

If more Black people knew this knowledge they

would not only have more self value, but they would not buy into the stereotypes of being poor, economically uneducated, or needing to be financially depended on the resources of others. Sadly theirs many Black people who know very little about history but they know who Julius Caesar is. Not enough know who Mansa Musa is and one can say he accomplished more in his lifetime than Caesar.

As stated earlier, a lot of Black people only learn their people's history from the standpoint of the oppression we historically face. This is not Black history in totality. We weren't always the victims to European colonialism. Before slavery in America, their were African kings and queens like Changamire Dumbo of Rozvi empire, Queen Nzingah of Ambundu Kingdom, Queen Amanirenas of Kush, and Sunni Ali all have successful reigns as rulers and all of which were successful in resisting colonialism whether diplomatically or through war. If more Black people knew these things, theirs a good chance they would have more of a sense of pride for their people. Such information however is rarely taught in schools.

Black people just happen to be living through an age of oppression, however every race has or will face its times of progress and regression for as long as humans are living on this earth. Despite your circumstances you can still decide to be a progressive Black person who will leave this world as a better place for the next generation regardless of the opposition you face.

If you knew your ancestors came from wealthy kingdoms and lands of an abundance of natural resources you would see Black oppression as just a period in history and not a permanent curse. The harsh truth is most of us will die in this age of oppression but we can still do the best we can to set the next generations up with the head start we never had. What do you want your legacy to be in our age of oppression? What do you want people to look back and say about your legend as you battled through this age of Black oppression? Did you help, be passive, or hinder the community you are apart of?

In order to be a helper of our community you must have knowledge of history which includes our slavery and oppression, but you must also know of your royalty and prosperity too. This means all Black people globally need to learn about their history outside of the educational system placed in front of us.

You should study books, videos, and independent classes / seminars, on Black history in totality. You will have to go and seek the knowledge and not expect it to come to you or to be told to you by a formal educational system. Most formal classes in school will only tell you about "American History" not the totality of who Black people have been on this earth. Black people should study things like the Kush Empire, the Moors, the Mali Empire, Rovzi Empire, Kemet, and ancient Egypt to name a few. Know stories like Queen Nzinga who was successful in ruling Angola and fought off the Portuguese until they gave up their conquest for the capture of slaves and land in her region. Black people need to know about the Moors who ruled Spain for 700 years giving the region advancements in education, technology and art that the region has not seen until that point. In fact many historians believe that it was the Moors rule in Spain that helped usher in The Renaissance which brough

Europe out of "The Dark Ages". Ironically formal education and textbooks will teach many that The Crusaders were the "good guys" although the Moors used very little force in the ruling of Spain and benefited the region more than they ever took from it.

Most people that I can think of who know Black history outside of the oppression of slavery and ideologies afterwards, not only seem to see Black people as valued beings to be preserved and protected, but they also seem to be more optimistic on what the community can accomplish. They also seem to take more action in the struggle against oppression instead of waiting for the solutions from others.

When you see the value in our times of prosperity, and our strength in more current years of oppression you will get a clearer understanding of the Black person you need to be for the community to prosper. Black people are not weak or inferior, we are not what negative stereotypes say we are, we are just currently living through our time of oppression. The good news is theirs plenty of examples of Black people achieving success anyways. Even in the face of systematic racism, slavery, and oppressive ideologies adopted by world powers thereafter.

Rapper/Activist David Banner, reminded us that we have been enslaved in America more than we've been free as a race collectively. This is correct as slavery lasted from the early 1500's to the 1860's followed by the "Jim Crow Era" lasting until the 1970's. Black people are the only race to overcome literacy oppression as their was a period and time during slavery where it was illegal to read and write. Although its barely mentioned in its proper context, Black people had an overall literacy turn over when it came writing, reading, and math, that this world has never seen.

Our history can be horrific in many times but theirs times of prosperity you must know of so you can see yourself as a descendants of a royalty not just the descendants of slaves. Although not every Black person's ancestors came to this country by slavery, when it came to the oppression thereafter slavery Blacks were equally yoked.

With the emergence of the internet and abundance of books of our history during our royalty and oppression, you have access to information that some of our ancestors didn't have access to. In this age of information at will, theirs no excuse not to know your own people's history outside of what school will teach. You can look up history on your phone just like you do anything else.

When a Black person has a broad perspective of their history chances are more than likely they will have a lot of pride in self, but will also look at other Black people more favorably instead of just another stranger. Knowledge can allow you to see yourself confidently not as stereotypes or how society would define you.

A Black person who is knowledgeable about the royalty in their people's history will not buy into the notion that black people are inherently poor, financially irrepressible, and unable to manage finances.

Knowing Black history will give you hope for your current circumstances because you will see struggle and pain, but you will also see that some of your ancestors prevailed in times and situations worse than yours. How can you doubt yourself in this world in 2023 when your ancestors had to overcome slavery, Jim Crow, and oppression to be great and successful?

When you study Black history in totality (as much as you can find) you will then gain pride in your race and culture which will make it easier for you to have pride in self. One has to have pride and belief in oneself first in order to see the same in other people.

Studying Black Leaders:

Theirs a population of Black people who are okay with knowing the Civil Rights leaders they learned from in school and nothing more. To limit your knowledge to what school or a formal education will teach you about is a limited recount of all the leaders and figures who helped shape a better today. Knowing about Martin Luther King Jr., Malcolm X, Rosa Parks, Fredrick Douglass and Harriet Tubman is very important, however a Black person should take the time to learn of more Civil Rights leaders and pioneers outside of school. This will be a continuous effort as theirs too many to be covered in any formal school curriculum.

Its difficult to know all of the people who were active in the advancement of Black people, however the thirst for knowledge in knowing what others before you have sacrifice is paramount to the success of the community. Finding and knowing the stories of Civil Rights leaders and those who fought for Black equality should be a life long journey of every Black person. Make sure you study less famous civil rights activist like Ella Baker, Stokely Carmichael, Fannie Hanmer, Reginald F. Lewis, and Dorthy Height. That's just a few, their many stories from others you should learn.

Many of the civil rights leaders in the past had to sacrifice freedom, their means of income, their reputations, their safety along with their family's safety, and in some cases their lives. All of this was so that their descendants could live a better quality of life. With the sacrifices that these people made for your betterment, its imperative that you know who these people are.

Going Beyond Formal Education:

Some formal institutions do not take the study of Black history as seriously as they could and some take the study very seriously, however only so many facts, people, and events can be taught in a semester, quarter, or school year. The study of the history and contribution of Black people is so vast only so much can be covered at schools who have the best of intentions in mind.

New historical facts come to the light of the stories of valor concerning Black historic figures and/or places of time. New information about who Black people are and what they have accomplished come to surface as time goes on.

To find more information about Black history you must read books that you may not find in school. Learn on the internet and searching for historical facts from trusted websites and reliable sources. Even if you are not an active learner, you can passively learn about Black historical figures and facts by following social media accounts that promote Black history.

When these accounts post on your timeline you can learn facts about your people without having to actively look for it. From time-to-time watch documentaries about historical Black figures, eras, and societies. Try searching for documentaries on subjects you are unaware of or could use more understanding of. Try to be just as entertained by learning about yourself and history just as much as you would for music, sports, and reality TV.

Leaders In Your Field:

Its extremely important for Black people to

know of the general leaders who have had a positive effect on our lives regardless of your walk of life. These would be people like Frederick Douglass and many others, whose work and action was beneficial to all Black people. It is very beneficial however to find prominent Black leaders who are in your field of work or area of interest. No matter what field you choose to go in, more than likely someone who looks like you achieved something in that area.

It's important to know what you will face not only as a professional in your desired field, you have to know what it is like to be a Black professional in that field. In some professions theirs obstacles you may run into regardless of race, however usually the Black perspective is different or unique in some type of way that others may not have to deal with.

Author and speaker Cyrus Ausar states perfectly how to look for the right leaders to motivate you in his book
"7 Steps To Discover Your Inner Greatness":

> *" In researching what you would love to do, start asking the, "who, what, where, when, and why?" Questions like: Who has achieved this goal before me? Where was this done? When did they do it, and in what time frame? Lastly, why did they do it?"*

A Black person should study the best Black person to do the job. Not only will you be prepared for what you may face, their stories may motivate you to keep going.

Book Sources:

The internet is a very powerful tool as far as sharing information however the most in depth information will come from books. Theirs an abundance of books that shares information on Black history and the study of our past and present conditioning.

One of my favorite books of all time is *Think And Grow Rich: A Black Choice* by **Napoleon Hill** and **Dennis Kimbro**. I recommend that every Black man and woman on earth should read this book at any age, but especially by the youth entering adulthood. This book outlines the stories and the overcoming of oppression that important Black figures had to endure to be successful.

Not only does this book share the story of these figures but it also explains what characteristics, traits, and actions that made them successful. It also tells the stories of past and more present figures in the passage, the book also gives excellent advice on how to be a better version of yourself. This book is a must read for all Black people.

Theirs plenty of books that are helpful for Black independence and prosperity. Some of the notable ones are *Powernomics* by **Dr. Claud Anderson**, which is a great read detailing how Black people were and still dealing economic racism, the impact of economic racism, and solutions to escape the grasp of poverty and dependency. Other notable books are *The Mis-Education of the Negro* by **Carter G. Woodson** which speak on the obstacles Black people have and will face in every area of life. The book discusses the psychological and mental affects of racism on the modern Black person and solutions of how to overcome such treatment.

Any book that is a biography or autobiography

of a prominent Black figure whether they are in business or excelled in their field of choice is worth reading. Always seek knowledge from Black people who have made it to a place prominence as they more than likely will tell you what hurdles they may have dealt with on journey. Any Black person in the pursuit of greatness may face obstacles that people of other races may not face.

Black History In The Schools:

Taking "Critical Race Theory" out schools means that a school curriculum will no longer teach African American history from a truthful and in-depth standpoint, censoring facts. I knew things were taking a turn for the worse when a teacher I know told me that some district text books in the state of Georgia referred to slaves as "laborers."

Theirs a clear difference between someone choosing to work (laborers) and someone who is forced to work free labor against their will (slave). Using a different choice of wording is a dramatic issue, as it tries to lighten the burden our ancestors truly went through. Trying to dilute the Black experience in America is a way to discredit what Black people truly went through, and to hide the atrocities that have happened to a race of people in the United States.

This is a scary thing because it shows that many in America have no true intentions on rectifying the past. If you cannot talk about and reflect on your past, then you have no intentions on fixing your future. Theirs a reason why a psychiatrist ask their patients about their past issues because hidden in the past are resolutions for the future.

Yet, if I'm being honest, students were getting a

watered-down version of Black history from formal schooling anyways. Most of which focuses on the same figures, fails to recognize the contributions of less popular figures, and speak of Black history from the standpoint of slavery or from the perspective of continually being a victim.

With the way things are trending, its more important than ever for Black people to educate themselves and their children at home and not to rely solely on what you learn in school. If you are a parent and feel like you don't know enough or are ignorant to Black history, you and your children can learn together.

Books From Others:

Books from Black authors will give you advice and wisdom of how to navigate life as a Black person, however that doesn't mean you cannot learn from non-Black authors. Notable books from others can still be helpful to Black people. Books like *The 4 Agreements* by **Don Miguel Ruiz,** *Power of the Subconscious Mind* by **Joseph Murphy,** *The 21 Irrefutable Laws of Leadership* by **John C. Maxwell, and** *48 Laws of Power* by **Robert Greene**, are good reads for anyone regardless of race. Of course, theirs way more books I could mention that will benefit you.

The Best Times To Read:

Nothing is wrong with reading a novel, or a science fiction story but everyone should read something that motivates them to be a better person. Reading a self-motivational book is beneficial to you no matter what time of the day you read it, however reading is even more beneficial in the morning when you first wake up and at night before you go to sleep. Your subconscious mind is most active when you first wake up and when you are about to go to sleep. What you do before you go to sleep and the first thing you do in the morning will set the tone for the rest of your day.

The subconscious mind influences the conscious mind and vice versa depending on the situation you are in. If you don't program your mind to think positive you will be at the mercy of whatever random feeling you may have at the start of the day, which can be positive or negative Programming your mind will influence you to think positive no matter what is going on.

"Man I just cant get into reading , I just don't have the time.."

Reading can be beneficial for you and your family for a lifetime, so regardless of if you like the practice of it or not, I'd make time for it. We all have the same 24 hours so you indeed DO have the time to read. The question is will you make the choice to read? Something as important as reading you should make time for. If you like watching TV, read passages from your motivational book during commercial breaks. When you go to restaurants or bars, take your book with you and read until your food comes out.

No matter what your method is make sure you set aside the time to read. Reading is nothing more than studying how to be a better self. The average millionaire reads 50 books a year. Of course, not all successful people read, but a good amount do. The answers to the majority of your problems can be found in books. Study the leaders to become a leader.

- Make it a lifestyle to learn as much about Black history until the day you take your last breath.

- Learn about Black history outside of and before Slavery.

- Learn about as many prominent Black kings, queens, leaders, and moguls throughout history.

- When learning of the horrors that Black people had to overcome throughout history, think with the mindset of coming from the linage of survivors NOT victims.

- Read as many books about Black history or the Black perspective on things.

- Share your newfound knowledge with others. Do NOT however, mock or look down on others for not knowing what you've just learned.

- If you are a parent make sure your children learn more about Black history and important Black figures than they will in the classroom.

- Make an effort to learn more about Black history than what you MAY learn in school.

- Study a successful Black figure that you never knew of before.

- Find Black leaders in your field of study both historic and present.

- Read as often as possible. Focus on reading books on self-development or leaders in your field of study.

WE WILL LOVE OURSELVES

Some understand the concept in having pride in oneself while others don't, and some *think* they have pride in self. Self-worth and self-confidence does not come from the things we have or can buy. Some Black people will fall for such a misconception and end up buying a lot of material things to increase their self-value. This is a false way of thinking and can be counter productive to you if it causes you to overspend on liabilities.

Most material things we can buy will one day break, fall apart, or get worn out. Will your self-worth dissipate along with those things? Money can make someone seem more valuable than they are, however, the money one possesses only defines them based on what they do with the money, not just having it.

Those who try to boost their self-esteem with money may find themselves purchasing expensive things to raise their worth for the sake of others. This could be the road to self-sabotage if your money is not spent and managed correctly.

When you have strong knowledge of self and value within, you will see yourself as valuable no matter how much money you have, and you won't talk about or want to see the downfall of others. In fact, you may tend to cheer for the success of others.

The Ideology of How Black People Are "Supposed" to Act:

In the corporate world, some people of color are so terrified of racial stereotypes that they may act outside of themselves to seek the approval of others. They may try to act in a manner in which others, non-Black people will find acceptable. The opposite is also true where some Black people will act in a manner that overly reinforces the stereotypes commonly associated with Black people. They may act too "ghetto" or act like they have no manners at all. Both of which are on the wrong path. First and foremost, what needs to be addressed in the Black community; ghetto does not always equal Black. This is something Black people and all people worldwide need to understand. We should not have to act ghetto to be considered Black, and we should not have to lose out cultural identity to be professional.

Black people should never have to act outside of themselves culturally to get an opportunity in the professional world, but we also do not have to live up to every single stereotype about the race either. One can keep their cultural identity and be successful however this also means that they don't have to live up all the notions and commonly held beliefs that others have came up with to define us. A Black person does not have to be the "White" person on the job, but they don't have to be the most ghetto person in the room either. True self-worth comes when you can be yourself, be proud of your culture, and live by principles that are important to you, not what others dictate as important to you. Black people can be very pro-Black yet respect others who are non-Black, all while not being ghetto or hood.

Value in Self:

The truth is your self-worth is your principals, your goals, your character, knowledge, and what you stand for. One should still have high value in self when everything is taken away from them. Who are you when you have nothing? Material things are additions in your life, they do not define you. They may display your style and taste but self-value cannot be bought. To have high self-value is understanding the principals you live by, loving yourself, knowing what you have to offer, and being honest enough with yourself to know what you have to work on to be better.

If you judge yourself on the material things you have, more than likely you are looking for the approval of others. Some may attach their self-worth to the tangible things others can see. Is someone worth more than you because they have more things than you? I hope not, because 9 times out of 10 theirs always someone who will have more than you.

One of the worst characteristics of some Black people who try to fill self-value voids with material things is they do so all so they can have one up on the next Black person who doesn't have the same things. This way of thinking is dangerous because it insists that one is only valuable base on the money and things they have. If this is a statement that rings true to you, than that means anyone who has more than *you* is more valuable than you. Never think this way, because value is deeper than what they eyes can see. You are better off looking at ones actions and character to determine value.

In fact I believe that if too much of your self worth is wrapped up in money you will end up being out leveraged by someone who has more money than you. You may even take on bad deals or situations looking at short term payment instead of looking at things from a long term perspective. That also means *you* also are no better than anyone else because of what you have.

Think More Than Money When Thinking Value:

Look inside yourself and see where your talents are and what your strong attributes are. What do you have to offer people? How can you help people? How does your character make you and other people better? When you are happy with yourself as a person and discover your self worth, you will value yourself whether you have a lot of money or not.

Why is valuing oneself without money important? The reason being is because no one knows what life will throw at them. You may be in a situation where you lose it all. All your money and all your material things. In order to recover from where you fell off, you will need to rely on your inner strength and self-worth to recover what you had and go beyond. Material items can be destroyed or worn out. Money can be destroyed, lost, stolen, or bank accounts can be compromised or frozen. The economy or stock market can take a dive. If any of these events were to happen, you do not want your self-worth to be tied to such things. If your self value is tied to the things you have, if you ever lose those things, you may think of yourself as worthless. Relying on the attributes you have outside of these things is what will help you recover.

When you don't discover your self-worth you may not see the value in yourself so you won't see it in others either. You run the risk of becoming a hater and try to devalue anyone who has less than you and discredit the validity or the worthiness of anyone who has more material things than you. You can become envious of people who have more than you and try to devalue them because what they have or accomplished makes you feel inferior. Since theirs always going to be someone who has less and more than you, its imperative that you see value in yourself and others outside of how much money or material possessions one has.

You will not be able to embrace your fellow brothers and sisters if your first reaction to people is to value them for what they do or do not have. You will encounter people thinking they have something to prove to you or you will assume they are worthless because you yourself need *something* tangible to make you feel worthy.

Always remember that Black ancestors after slavery, reconstruction, and Jim Crow had very little and were considered poor and illiterate. Yet many Black people from these circumstances were able to make something out of themselves and live prosperous lives. Would you negatively judge your ancestors for making something from nothing? If you are wise, you won't. The same respect you would give to the ancestors who supported families with very little should be shown to your peers in present times. If you have an abundance of material things and money, make sure you are helping others achieve their best selves along the way.

- Understand that your self-value should not be tied to the material possessions you have. Not even money alone should determine your self-value.

- Do NOT judge others only on the material things they have or the money they possess.

- If you must judge someone, judge them on their character, their attitude, their results, and how they treat others.

- Take the time and write a list of all the things that make you valuable outside of the material things you have.

- Think of someone who is rich and famous and write down all the ways in which they are valuable without mentioning money or material possessions.

- Think of someone who is not rich maybe someone you know personally, and write down all the ways in which they are valuable excluding money or material possessions.

- Do NOT engage in conversations that judge people based off of superficial means. Have the discernment to differentiate between those who are joking in such conversations and those who speak seriously of ones need for material possessions to be valuable.

- Avoid those who speak envious because of what others have.

WE WILL FIND OUR INNER STRENGTH

I'm 100 percent a black man. I recognize the God in me. Doing so allows me to ignore the social norms that consciously and subconsciously tell me I'm inferior because of my race gender, or class.

-Charlamage Tha God/ Black Privilege

Some think that when certain things happen for them, then they will discover happiness. Some believe "If I get all the money I want I will be happy" which isn't true. Theirs some rich people who are unhappy and some have even committed suicide with riches. The truth is happiness comes from within whether you are rich or poor. Inner happiness comes then success, not the other way around.

To put it simple, those who are happy with themselves and know their self worth for the most part tend not to be haters, aren't as judgmental, and don't feel like everyone has to prove or validate something to them.

Black people have been so afflicted by the horrors of oppression that some have poor self-worth from a subconscious standpoint whether we admit it or even know it. Our actions will always show how we truly value ourselves regardless of the words we speak. Some will have good rhetoric and seem confident because of how they speak of themselves but the question we should all ask, "Would I still have value in self without (fill in the blank)?"

Believing in the right principals and having good characteristics can be enough to know your self-worth. Find out what you love to do or what you are good at and see how it can benefit your life whether it becomes a job or a hobby. The more internal happiness you have inside the less likely you are to spend your energy bringing others down. How we view ourselves is usually how you will look at others. When you look for value in yourself beyond what you have, you will tend not to judge others on superficial means like the car a person drives or the outfit they have on.

Principles are something can be learned from parents, teachers, friends, religions, motivational people, and books. It will be up to you to differentiate what principles you will apply to your life and which ones you will ignore. If you don't know where to start you can start with the *Golden Rule: "Treat others how you would like to be treated."*

Do you want to be judged, hated on, and talk about before others can get to know you? Do you want to be judged on what you don't have? If you answer is *"no"* then you can start by not doing these things to other people. A Black person's respect and admiration should not be limited to the people they know and/or the famous people they have admiration for. When you are happy internally it does not mean you are going to agree with everything and everyone, but it means you won't be a hater of someone who is different than you.

Happy people want to spread happiness and joy to others while haters want to spread judgement towards others. Which of the two positions do you want to have in life? Will you be a spreader of hate or a spreader of love? Be warned: The same energy you give to others the universe will give that same energy to you. Happy people will see the good qualities in people and speak on them while haters will always talk about what one is lacking. Happy and positive thinking will give you more things to be happy and positive about while hating and negative thinking will give you more things to hate and the time will come for others to hate on you.

Do Not Let Stereotypes Define You-

Your brain is like a magnate attracting whatever you put in your subconscious whether good or bad. Having a broad sense of history when it comes to Black people can help you see yourself and others like you as valuable and not just limiting stereotypes as your frame of reference.

One reason many Black people may look to material things for self-value is because the world may be telling them they are "poor" or "unworthy" so the first thing some Black people strive out to do is to prove otherwise. Unfortunately, this may cause some to seek expensive things of materialistic value, so that others value them, or even so they can value themselves. Some will do this even if they cannot afford expensive materialistic things. Some will take on liabilities to impress others.

Black Self Value May Take Some Time...Be Patient-

Black people collectively have been in slavery or having to deal with life as a third-class citizen longer than they have been free. This means the collective will have to be patient and even see the great possibilities in their people even if the reality we face seems bleak presently. The race should be a collective of people who are willing to build up and encourage those who are lacking in self-esteem.

In order for us to embrace one another many of us will have to put the ways of a hater behind us and see great potential in one another. Another person's value shouldn't make you feel inferior because we all are valuable in some way. It's up to you to find it, understand it, hone it, and use it to eliminate the doubt you may have in yourself.

A hater lives with a lot of self-doubt whether they admit it or not, which is evident because they are always worried about what someone else is doing. They always seem critical about the flaws of others yet fail to realize that all people have flaws including themselves. Be patient when discovering your own value in self, and when you do this, be patient with others who are also looking for their own value in self.

Your aim should be to understand where you can be a person of value. It is vital that you understand where you can be of more value in a given area than your average person. We all have above average talent at something that makes us unique from one another. Identifying what your talents are, where your strengths are, or what you have a lot of knowledge in can be one of the most useful tools in your arsenal that can benefit you for a lifetime.

Find Your Talent-

It benefits one to find out what they are good at or what they like to do so it can enrich their lives either as a form of income or just a hobby for therapeutic purposes. Your talents and skills are usually more valuable than the money you have or things you have. The reason for this is because material things don't last, money comes and goes but usually your talents can last you a lifetime.

Use Your Talents As A Form of Income-

When you discover what you are talented at or what you are skilled in, it can give you a good idea of the career or jobs you should focus on. You can find your talents through way of self-evaluation. What do you do at a level that is higher than the average person? What do others say you are good at? If you are a teenager reading this book you can find jobs that are closely related to your talent or if you are going to college you can declare a major closely related to your talent.

You can use your talents as a form of income or you can base your career around that talent. Theirs a good chance that in this life you will spend more time at work than with your family and friends, so whatever you do for a living, you are a lot better off doing something that you love.

As a Black person, having as many forms of income is a way of safety and protection, as a good amount of Black people will work for companies owned by others or the government where their income can be compromised at any time for any reason. Even if a Black person works for a Black owned company theirs no guarantees in the work force. The majority of the jobs available are not 100% secure, which means we all need other forms of income, even if you absolutely love your job.

This life will test you with as many hardships and difficult situations from time to time and no one on this earth is immune. With this being the case, you want to give yourself as many advantages in life as possible, because tough times are going to come.

You give yourself an advantage when you base a form of income around something you are good at, something you are passionate about, and or something you have a lot of knowledge of. As stated earlier there's no guarantees that things will work in your favor, but theirs a good chance you will fight harder to establish something around something you love. As for me I always struggled to work jobs I did not enjoy, if you are the same, be selective with the work you choose.

Using Your Talent Just For Fun-

Some may fear that using their talents for work or income can take the passion or fun out of what they love. You may want to just keep your talent as a hoppy that you do for fun outside of work, which is perfectly fine. You may use your talent for therapeutic means to relieve stress or to be entertained in a constructive way.

Using your talent to relieve stress is just as important as using your talents to make money. We all need a healthy escape from work and better it be a hobby than drugs, addictions, or bad habits. Having something that you love to do is good for fighting off stress, depression, and may give your life meaning if what you do for work doesn't.

"How does finding your talents break Black barriers?"

Theirs many ways that our talents can help people bond with one another. The ugly truth is people tend to value others more when they have a talent (I'm talking from personal experience on this). People who may not have seen value in you before they knew of your talent(s) will see it now. People will tend to treat you with more respect when they see your talents. Of course, others should see us for more than what we are talented at, however theirs no denying the truth of human nature. We value the talents attached to the person sometimes even more than the person themselves.

When you and another person share the same talent, it can be a way for you to connect and relate to one another. Friendship and meaningful relationships can be fostered more easily when you share the same hobby as someone else. You can not only relate to one another, but you can learn from each other and build better things together than you could as individuals. You could also be the missing link in someone's business. You may have the talent that can make you valuable which will add to your monetary gain. You could be the asset someone needs in a situation where you both can benefit from.

Most importantly we are all examples to someone. Whether we are an example for our own children/ family members, friends, people outside of our family, or people we don't know. We can either be a good example or a bad example.

Your skills may inspire people younger than you to go the same route or even do things better than how you are doing it. You can inspire your family members or even peers to take on the same talent or for them to use their own talents in the same way that you do. Whether its social media, coworkers, or people you don't know personally, you may inspire people you don't know, all by your example.

- Understand that you are a valuable person. Its up to you to find what your value is and leverage it.

- Realize that you do not have to be attached to anything to be valuable.

- Find what you are good at, passionate about, and/or have a lot of knowledge in.

- Decide whether you are going to create income for your talents or just use it as a hobby.

- Hone your skills. You are an example to people know and those you don't.

- Share the knowledge you have in your craft with others.

- Whether it's for monetary gain or just a hobby, do what makes you happy.

WE WILL ACKNOWLEDGE OUR NATURAL BEAUTY

You must have self-love to harbor good relationships with other Black people. Love for self extends beyond inner self-value you must love the exterior, your body. Every Black person should love how they look naturally. We need no modifications or add ons at all to be beautiful, which applies to both men and women.

One should care more about how they feel about themselves and less how others feel about them. Nothing's wrong with being presentable or good looking for others, however it should not come at the expense of your self-esteem.

Be clean, neat, and presentable, but never feel like you have to alter yourself for others. Every woman should think of themselves as beautiful and every man should think of himself as handsome without anyone's validation. Having high self-worth is knowing that you don't need anyone's validation simultaneously, you must also realize others do not require your validation either.

You Are Good Enough As You Are:

Black people currently and historically have had very little control over most of the industries or distribution of the media, which at the time gave our generations of that time a White or European standard of beauty.

For Black women it would mean rejecting natural hair for straight long hair (whether theirs or additions by weave) and for our men it would mean straightening their hair which was a phase that did not last as long for Black men as it did for Black women. Black men's change of hair may not have lasted as long as it did for Black women however some Black men refused to accept Black women in their natural state. Many would prefer how a black woman should look to societies standards.

In the late 1960 and the 1970's we would see a large majority of Black people embrace natural hair styles like the afro. Somehow for whatever reason by the 1980's the masses of Black people (not all but a good majority) reverted back to the embracing the idea of straight hair or add on weave with a Black twist to it. Even though Black men did not face as much stigma for their hair, even in present times at some places of work, locs are considered *unprofessional.* From my experience, many of Black men at that time would prefer straight hair over a Black woman's natural hair. In the new millennium (year 2000 and beyond) I'm glad to see the progress that women have made in accepting who they are and the approval of many of our men with the natural hair movement we are living through. However some are still divided on the issue and prefer or older view of beauty or how a black woman *should* look.

"Whats wrong with wearing weave or getting a relaxer? Its just hair!"

This is true so lets be clear, both Black women who have long straight hair, wear weave, and have natural hair are all equally beautiful. A distinction has to be made however. Theirs Black women who may wear weave from time to time and then theirs women who cannot live life without weave. And for those who cannot live without it are those who need to be addressed.

No judgment is being passed here because

many women may have not only gotten their standard of beauty from the media but their parents who themselves were influenced by the media's standard of beauty directly or indirectly. Some things are harder to change when they are passed down from generation to generation.

In America for most of the last century Black women were only seen as professional if they wore European based hair styles. This meant for Black women straight hair was acceptable and natural styles like an afro, locks, and for a time even curly hair in general was seen as unprofessional until recent times. In fact it wasn't until the 21st century where companies were no longer allowed to discriminate by hair choice. With these things in mind we have to make sure to be patient and kind when deal of this subject matter.

In order to find your beauty you may even have to go against your own parents standard of beauty. I am a man, and I also know that women are held to a higher standard of beauty and men are and are judged more on the basis of their looks than men are. With this in mind, Black men must make it a point to make all of our women feel beautiful and not just the ones we are attracted to.

For me honestly, I think Black women are most beautiful with their natural hair. It doesn't matter if you are bald or have a head full of hair, you are beautiful and our men are ready to acknowledge your beauty regardless of what societies standard is. I'd assume its not healthy for ones scalp to be buried under a wig/weave for weeks/months on end, or for acid to put on your head all just to make your hair straight. The beauty standards for Black women should never come at the expense of their health.

When my mom had to have operations done

due to the number of relaxers, she's had over the years I became a strong opposer of hair straightening chemicals. No look or style is worth the expense of your health.

Realizing the Beauty Within-

Can a woman wear a wig or weave and have high self-esteem and self-worth? Yes, of course! However, the question that all Black women of all ages and backgrounds must ask themselves :*"Am I beautiful it"?* What you think of yourself is and will always be most important. I personally know some women who would not like to be seen with their natural hair.

If they have to go somewhere with their natural hair they would prefer to put on a bonnet or a scarf, yet feel more presentable when they have synthetic hair added to what they have or that their hair be modified by chemicals. Why is it that some women value what they add or change about their hair, but dislike how it naturally is? I'd like for these kind of women to have high esteem with their natural hair jus as much as when they alter it.

Black men should not insist that our women change their hair other than its natural state to be *"acceptable"*. This is an issue that many older Black men struggle with but must be addressed. We need to continue to encourage our women to accept what they are presently without modification. Black men however should not look down on women who wear weave, fake hair, or relaxers. We have to remember a standard of beauty has been handed down from generation to generation and it may take some Black women longer than others to discover high self-esteem of oneself in a natural state.

Black men have to be patient and encouraging. We have to remember that sometimes women wear wigs and weave for reasons we may not be aware of. Some women may have loss hair due to a chronic illness or disorder and may not be ready to face the world bald yet, which is more than understandable. Ladies in these situations when you are ready to come out into the world as you truly are, you will still be beautiful. Black women are beautiful no matter what the length of their hair is or texture.

I love Black women no matter what the hair style of choice however I would be joyous of the day when all black women wear their natural hair no matter what the length is. Women who embrace addon hair products are beautiful and worthy as well, I just want to encourage women to feel just as beautiful when they don't have these things. In 2023 we as a people do a better job at acknowledging our natural beauty. The goal is to not only maintain but to expand this movement and encourage others so we can pass a new *"standard of beauty"* for the next generations to come.

Men Accepting Natural Self:

If we are talking about hair Black men, you are not off the hook! In a interview with *The Breakfast Club Power 105,* rapper/activist David Banner spoke of how he let his grey hair show. "The grey hair lets youth know that they are around an elder." One thing I've noticed from men of all races is that many fear getting older or being an elder, some want to be young forever. Its personified when trying to appear to being younger than you truly are.

Many men fear getting older because they think

of slowing down, getting weaker, or losing libido. It shows up both mentally and physically. The truth is if you live a healthy lifestyle these are things that you don't have to worry as much about. Some however are not disciplined enough to live a healthy lifestyle. Others may just go grey sooner than they'd like so they dye their hair to look younger.

Oddly enough most women that I know actually find grey hair on a man to be attractive. Some men go bald before they'd like to. They may color in bald spots, or even get a hair unit installed (fake hair for men). I bring these things up because its unfair for Black men to demand that Black women accept their natural selves if we don't.

The diaspora of Black men must embrace their age. It's a blessing to grow older. Some don't decline because they gotten older, some decline because of their lifestyle choices. For the community to flourish Black men cannot be afraid to grow older. If we want our women to embrace who they are, we have to embrace who we are.

Finding inner beauty is not just subjected to Black women but Black men also have to find what beauty is outside of societies standards. Men in general do not have the same societal pressure to be beautiful as women do, however Black men still have to deal with an ideology of having to add something to themselves to be accepted not only in general society but even in the Black community. Many of Black men may feel the pressure from society and even their own people to give in to consumerism as way to elevate self-value. Some Black men don't feel whole if they do not have on the right clothes by the right brand.

Having any car is a blessing however some

Black people feel as though they are better if they have a certain brand of car. Some men are car enthusiast and love certain cars from an enthusiast standpoint. However, there's also some who want a certain brand of car all because they know it will boost their value in the eyes of others. Men who think this way, seem to attach their value to what they can buy or show others. This screams insecurity, however societal ideologies make this way of thinking normal for a lot of people.

Black men must know and understand their value beyond what they can buy or put on their body. All too often I have witnessed Black men being ridiculed by their peers about the brand of shoes or clothes that they have on which is ironic because theirs many wealthy people who could care less about these things. A difference in style should be seen as unique. Black people shouldn't live in a world where we all have to wear certain brands and own certain brands to be accepted.

No doubt joking around is apart of Black culture. We can no doubt joke about each other without placing the worth of Society may have gave us such an ideology but that does not mean we have to abide by it.

All Black people have great things to offer this world. To subject a Black person's value to what they own or have is no different than saying they would be worthless if they don't own certain material objects. Are Black people only as valuable as the things they own or add to themselves? Does our value have to be brought from a store? When you understand value in self you will realize that you are good enough and anything you buy is just an addition, but what you buy alone does not define you.

How Does This Break Barriers Among Black People? :

The way we treat others is usually a mirror. How we perceive others is usually how we perceive ourselves. The standard you hold for yourself you usually hold for others as well. If you feel like you need to add something to yourself to be worthy, then you will feel the same way towards others. You can find yourself being judgmental towards others because you are constantly judging yourself. When you can see value in yourself outside of what you can add on or buy, you will allow the same for others.

When we can value each other outside of alterations or consumerism barriers that divide the community fall. When we strive to see value in each other outside of consumerism, we force ourselves to see value in others beyond superficial means. Any manner of people with the right money can buy things of "value" but those who have internal value, those things cannot be bought. People have to develop and nurture their characteristics and no matter the social status of a person, this is a truer indication of who this person is and not what they bought.

The goal of this book is to get Black people to respect each other, work together, and love each other. None of these things can be done if we judge each other based on superficial means. They say "don't judge a book by its cover" which is so true, yet sadly many do this anyways. Some of the best books I've ever read did not have a fancy cover, in fact many of which had a basic mediocre cover at best. It wasn't until I cracked open and read books that I found the true value in them. When I read a good book, I get so intrigued by to content in the book, that I care less about the cover.

Speak Positive: What You Say Matters

The words you say to yourself are very important, don't underestimate it! The words we speak influence our confidence, our emotions, and our physical/mental health. I believe like many that the words we speak even influence our future as well.

A problem that a lot of people have is they are only influenced by their current circumstances. They can't fathom things getting better until they do. They cannot envision better circumstances. They do not choose to be happy; they wait for outside circumstances to make them happy.

For many when they think negative, so they talk negative. This negative talk can range from self-doubt, being judgmental of self, and denying the possibility of positive results. They say negative things about themselves to themselves and sometime aloud.

If this is you, the good thing is you can always change your ways and speak positive words. I'm a testament that if you speak positive words to yourself it will come into your reality. Even if you don't believe in the laws of attraction, or positive affirmations, simply restating what you want to yourself is a reminder of what you want to focus on. You put your energy and effort into what you focus on.

- Look yourself in the mirror and tell yourself positive affirmations every morning like: "I love you", "I'm more than enough", "I'm a beautiful person". You can come up with your own affirmations.

- Understand that you are valuable and worthwhile without adding anything to your being.

- Do NOT judge others solely on what they do or do not have.

- See the value in others who do not have fancy things or material possessions.

- How you judge yourself is how you will judge others, make sure you have a loving relationship with yourself.

- Do not take the judgement of others personally. Some are projecting their insecurities onto you. Do not fall for it.

- Value more of the content of one's character, their attitude, and the way they treat others more than what they have.

WE WILL ACCEPT
EACH OTHER

When some Black people have issues of accepting themselves, it is even harder for some not to stick negative stereotypes on their own people. Our differences are to be celebrated, not to be mocked for what society says a Black person should be. Differences in opinion, principles, and ideologies are to be debated with one another not argued with.

The fact that you are interacting with someone who shares the same racial issues in this world should override any differences of opinion, beliefs, and origin. Before you and the other person learned what you both believe in today, you were both Black first. The world may have their own opinion or stereotype of how Black people "should" be, that does not mean we have to embrace or follow these ideas. We can reject them and set our own standards.

Black people are just like any race people where theirs a variety of us and we all don't fit into what stereotypes say we are. Some may live up to common stereotypes but that doesn't mean the entire race has to meet up to popular generalization in order to be a Black person.

"So we just supposed to get along with everyone? Don't we have to draw the line somewhere, a standard?"

There's a difference between not agreeing with someone and hating them. People who have different personalities, characteristics, and life experiences will all develop their own ideas, actions, and principles on life. It's understandable that you will not get along with everyone and some people are toxic to you. If you must distance yourself from a fellow Black person, let it be because of a lack of respect, flaws in character, negative actions, and regressive principles, NOT differences in religion, political views, ideologies, culture, mannerism, or sexual orientation.

Before you distance yourself from your peers try to consider their point of view and where they are coming from. If a resolution cannot be found among one another, you can simply not deal with each other without having to drag the other person through the mud. No matter what the disagreement is a Black person should never want to see another Black person fail.

The best scenario is to celebrate and embrace each other's differences for the sake of building stronger communities and networking circles. The fact that many Black people can't put personal beliefs asides to work with people different from them, shows that we must be loyal to our *"Blackness"* before any personal or societal belief. We shouldn't have to agree on everything to communicate, network, and build relationships with each other.

Reserve your judgment for actions, character, and principles. The fact that Black people globally share systematic racism is a commonality worth uniting with each other no matter what ideologies we adhere to.

Where To Draw the Line On Acceptance:

A community has to have some type of standard of course. Not all mean well in the community, and it is those who we should be weary of. Before we judge each other, we need to be a loving community that allows our people to grow. Even us, who are well inform and well educated were once ignorant and did not have the same capacity of knowledge that we have now. Theirs a good majority of Black people who will grow in a single-family home. Some of which will be in environments where the single parent works more than they are able to interact with their children.

Some may grow up fast in such environments which may cause them to mature faster than most their age. In this fast growth some may miss valuable lessons along the way. They may be misled into learning toxic traits from their peers their age without guidance to tell them otherwise. Either way we must practice patience with our people and understand for some, it can take longer for them to mature. Yet and still a standard for Black people must be established.

The diaspora should take a stand against those who do negative actions against the community for profit or disdain. We should have no tolerance for people who sell-out, bring negativity, bring violence and or death to the community. Ones Blackness and acceptance in the community should not come down to, how someone talks, what neighborhood they are from, or their area of interest.

Ironically some will say someone is Blacker than someone else because they encompass a walking stereotype. Even if they do nothing good for the Black community or even worse bring negativity and or death to the community. Some can be considered more Black depending on how hood or ghetto they are. If someone has a great deal of knowledge, and helps the Black community, to some those things alone are not enough to establish their blackness.

If you don't live up to the stereotypes your Blackness comes into question. Other races are free to think like this, but when Black people adopt this way of thinking, its sad, and does nothing good for our community. These same people will vilify sellouts or Black people who align with the ideology of other races, yet refuse to take responsibility for their part in pushing Black people away who don't live up to the "nigga" stereotype.

We should discard those who harm the community, and not the ones who don't live up to the stereotype of how Black people are supposed to act. We must understand the difference between having a standard and accepting each others differences. When we can distinguish the difference between the two barriers in the community will fall.

Accepting Each Other's Differences-

Acceptance and agreements are two different things, however many people get the two words mixed up. Agreeing with someone means you share or believe in the same concept as they do. Accepting someone is embracing one regardless of what they believe in. The problem is many operate from a place of agreement instead of acceptance. When this happens Black people find themselves divided over issues that aren't important as far as community growth.

Religion is understandably important for us individually but in my opinion, you should care less about what someone else believes in. In all reality the Black community is oppressed and does not have room for division if we are to grow as a community. As stated in previous laws nothing wrong with religion being a significant factor in

YOUR life, however I do not believe it is ok to distance yourself from others solely because they may have different beliefs. Looking at the bigger picture, we are at a place where we must put our differences aside to work together.

Be less concerned with one's sexual orientation and more concerned with how they take care their family. Be less concerned with where someone is from and more concerned about where they are going in life. Be less concerned with someone's political stance, and more concerned with what a person does for his/her community. When we let general societal concepts tell us how we as a people should judge ourselves and others, we allow others to create a narrative of what is acceptable in our community.

Black people can do great things together if we are willing. Would you pass up on a business opportunity or a chance to make a lot of money because the person you are dealing with is gay? Or would you pass up an opportunity because someone doesn't practice the same religion? Would you not do what's beneficial for your community because you are working with someone of opposite political beliefs? If so, you could be hindering the growth of yourself and your community.

Black people being different and having differences is a great thing. It is going to take Black people from multiple walks of life to elevate the entire community. If someone does something that benefits the community who cares about their religion, where they are from, sexual orientation, or what political party they are affiliated with.

When Black people accept each other's differences, it will allow for more variety when it comes to businesses, opportunities, and community development. If the Black community has the same thoughts and ideas, in some ways it can work well, but it can also be detrimental. If everyone has the same ideas on everything it can cause the community to lack in areas of importance because of a lack of diversity.

Communities should be like an ecosystem in nature. Most successful ecosystems have a variety of animals, plants, and insects whom of which have different functions but are equally important and equally reliant on one another. Insects help plants pollinate, herbivores eat the plants, and carnivores eat the herbivores. All of which are important in the development of an ecosystem. If one area is off balance, it can cause the deterioration of an entire ecosystem, and some species may die out altogether. Black people have everything to gain coming together, they have nothing to gain when divided.

Love Each Other Despite Differences vs Societal Norms:

Nothings wrong with Black people having a code or agreed standard, but in reality, we are not going to all agree on everything or have the same interest. The true question is do we have to agree or even understand each other to love each other? I'd say no. I am using love in the context of wanting to see one do well in life and wishing them no harm, not in the closer way you would regard to a friend or significant other. A type of love you could have for a stranger or someone you disagree with. I can reject their ideology and still see them as a person.

Another truth is you can still do good business and network with people who have different interests and ideologies than you. As a people who are oppressed globally, we should put our opinion aside in regard to how others choose to live their lives. When doing business, the main concern should be value, results, character, dependability, and experience. Things like religion, sexual orientation, ideologies on how relationships should be, and/or how a family structure should be running are all things that can be figured out if you grow closer to someone.

We do not have the luxury of being divided because we think differently or have different values. If a Black person were to be seen in court Id imagine they'd get judged the same way whether they are gay or straight. If a Black person were to get stopped by the police, I'd imagine he could get viewed the same way whether he is religious or atheist. An appraiser may not undervalue your home because of what neighborhood you are from, what state you were born in, or what country you are from, but they just might just because you are Black.

We need to realize that we face the same injustices no matter what ideologies we arere to. During World War I when soldiers were in foxholes, they could depend on each other and I'm sure they could care less about what the other person believes in. The agenda is survival and victory; everything else can be figured out later. When Black people can think on this level, we can break down the barriers we created to divide ourselves.

A Black person has the right to be unique just like people of any other race. Sure being "different" can naturally make you a subject of ridicule and speculation no matter what your race is. However, in the African American community being "different" can cause others to attempt to strip you of your racial identity. Do not let others deter you from being yourself and all Black people should keep in mind what **Robert Greene** wrote in his book *48 Laws of Power*. In *Law 25 Re-Create Yourself* he wrote the following:

" *Do not accept the roles that society foists on you. Re-create yourself by forging a new identity, one that commands attention and never bores the audience. Be the master of your own image rather than letting others define you. Incorporate dramatic devices into your public gestures and actions- your power will be enhanced and your character will seem larger than life.* "

Understanding Our Fight:

I remember watching HBO series *Band of Brothers*, a show about U.S. soldiers in Germany during World War II. While at war the soldiers functioned well together. Some may have had psychological issues, some may have had disagreements, but whenever in conflict they functioned like a well-oiled machine for the most part.

When the war was won, however, and soldiers were waiting to go home but still deployed in Europe. This is when all the trouble happened. The soldiers had so much free time on their hands that they started to engage in mischievous acts. In one episode a soldier got drunk and shot and killed a fellow soldier.

Even in the movie *Jarhead* a movie about the psychological affects of war set in the 1990's during Operation: Desert Storm. During times of combat, the units functioned well, but when the down time came that's where the issues, disfunction, and again mischief arose. In fact, in one scene one soldier had a rifle pointed directly in fellow soldier's face because one of the soldiers got the other one in trouble. During times of live action combat in the movie however, such a thing never took place.

When soldiers are in conflict, they don't have time to bicker or ague among each other whose way of life is right or better. Things of which are put aside to work together for the common goal of survival and achieving an objective. When we realize we are at war we will put our differences aside for a greater good. But if we have a mindset where we don't realize we are at war, we will think we have the luxury of separation, judgement, and even turning against one another.

Black people around the globe are soldiers in the same uniform and in the same foxhole whether they know it or not. How you want or think things are can be totally different from what the reality truly is. Just like war, your beliefs on things do not take you out of the foxhole. The only thing that will get you all out of there alive is teamwork, survival, and victory. When Black people truly take on the scope of what we have against us we will realize how much we need each other despite our differences.

Our Differences Give Us Power:

For the Black community to prosper, we must have people work and succeed in a variety of fields, not just the ones popularly associated with the community. We should be proud of our community members who are making big strides in the areas of entertainment and sports. However the community needs a Black person to be successful in all areas of life. Just as we need Black actors we also need Black scientist, just like we need Black athletes we also need Black farmers, and just as we need Black musicians we also need Black owners of energy sources.

The question becomes however, how do we foster a community of people to do different things when we demand that Black people all walk, talk, and think the same? In order to have a wide net of people succeeding in multiple areas, it's going to take a variety of people with different interests. Our community must allow for people who have interests that are different than what stereotypes suggest we should be concerned about.

Our variety will give us more power going forward. If we are going to have Black representation in areas that we did not represent before, its going to take Black people with interest that may be different from the norm. Where do you stand on this? Are you one of those people who limit Blackness to popular stereotypes? If you are, I suggest you change your ways because that way of thinking stunts the growth of the Black community.

Where We Draw the Line:

One of the hardest things to accept as a Black person is you may have to distance yourself from people who look like you. Some do not mean you well and will bring negativity in your life.

Excluding someone should be a last resort but it should be used in extreme circumstances when your core values, and livelihood are threatened. If being around this person lowers your quality of life, you must distance yourself from them.

The wrong people can be like a magnet bringing negativity to your life. Simply being in their proximity you can become collateral damage when negativity comes. You must preserve yourself for yourself and so you can be of service to others.

People who continually hurt you, don't respect your boundaries, and make your life worse are people you need to get rid of. Be sure to voice the issues you have with people. Some may change their ways when you bring it to their attention. If they don't burn the bridge.

- Accept the differences others have and realize it will take a variety of people for the Black community to grow.

- The community should reject those whose actions harm the community NOT reject those who don't live up to stereotypes.

- Understand that in some cases you and others should put your differences aside for the betterment of the community.

- Division in the community weakens the community.

- Variety in the community is strength in the community.

- Broaden your horizons and realize for community independence we need Black people succeeding in every area of life.

- Accept others who look like you but have other interest and ideologies.

- Understand the concept that I can still value and respect someone although we do not agree on certain things.

- Realize that business and networking can be done with people who think differently than you. Be careful not to burn the wrong bridge. Someone you don't agree with on personal things can be an asset in business.

- Other races and society can choose to follow the ideas of division and separation because of ideologies, but Black people should NOT do the same practice.

- Remember that a good community is like a good ecosystem with a variety of animals. Allow for the Black community to have variety and don't narrow others down to what you think they should be.

- Understand that almost every component in society is geared to work against Black people, we should function like we at war and work together. We can worry about our differences after victory.

- If you were a person who divided yourself from someone because they were different than you make it a point to apologize.

- If you are a parent, raise your children to see value in people they disagree with.

WE WILL RESPECT ALL GENERATIONS

One of the biggest issues in the Black community is the lack of respect and value in each other from generation to generation. The community itself suffers from inner ageism which has and will continue to work against the progress of the entire race.

Since many of the common present-day stereotypes of young Black people are negative, many older Black people from earlier generations buy into these notions and then feel as if these ideas are confirmed when a select few act out these stereotypes. On the other side of the spectrum some of the younger generations are completely oblivious to the sacrifices generations before them have made.

Some of the younger generations of Blacks can even view their elders as weak for the oppression the community collective suffered, or may think of them as weak minded for buying into things like politics and religion. Some youth may feel like the stories or the lessons that the elders have don't matter. Some of the elders may see younger people as ignorant, lazy, and incompetent. Both sides accept generalizations about Black people that were not set by Black people.

The truth is all generations of Black people can learn from each other from the eldest to the youngest as the community collectively can benefit from the knowledge of the past, present, and future. The youth should look to the elders with respect as they most likely endured a world and tougher times than we enjoy today. They had to make major sacrifices for younger Black people to have the opportunities they have in present day.

The respect must go both ways however. The elder generations must respect the youth, as they are dealing with a constantly evolving world in which they need guidance and encouragement from their elders not constant hostility and judgement. Ironically elder Black people will need the guidance of the youth because the world is changing in ways that can be unfamiliar to them. Young Black people are the gate keepers to the progression of the collective and should be treated as such. Neither group should look at each other with negative expectancy.

Both parties, younger and older generations should show each other respect first before having to prove they are worth respecting. The elders can share history to help the youth so they can know what they need to fight for to benefit the present and the future. The elders need the youth to keep the older generations up to date as far as current events, new technology, and up to date information on the world we are living in. A wise person takes on both new and old perspectives.

My Experience:

Our society in general struggles with the idea of looking at other generations with respect regardless of race. I've seen this as an issue for the Black community as long as I've been alive (35 years). Some from the younger generations can seem to be fixated only on present day issues and some of which can be blissfully ignorant to important and historical issues in favor of pop culture.

Its to my surprise, theirs a population of younger generations of Black people who could care less about seeking the knowledge and stories of those who sacrificed for them to have the opportunities that many enjoy today. All Black millennials MUST know Black history beyond what is told in school so they can know how to be effective in their future works and ideas.

The problem I see with older generations is once again some of them, generalize younger people with negative stereotypes. Instead of judging young people on an individual basis, they will throw anyone who is young into the generalized stereotypes concerning millennials without getting to know them on a personal level. I've heard numerous conversations from people who are generations above me talk negatively about the entire generation of millennials.

Some of the negative stereotypes concerning the younger generations is that they are lazy, obsessed with technology, not makers of good music, oblivious to the past, and oblivious to important issues. Other stereotypes are that the younger generation is soft, unmotivated, and or lacking skills that were essential in previous times. Do some younger people fall under these stereotypes? Yes of course, but do all younger people fall under these stereotypes? NO! Theirs many of millennials who do have knowledge of the past, who are trying to make a better future, and who leverage technology to make them wiser, and better instead of being controlled by it.

Both elder generations and younger generations have something meaningful and beneficial that can be taught to one another. The Black community will gain great things when we listen, learn, and care for one another. Dealing with all the oppression in this world Black people need knowledge from the past and the present to have a better future collectively.

Bringing The Generations Together:

For The Younger Generations-

In 2023 and beyond we have super computers at our fingertips called "smart phones." Most millennials have cell phones in which they keep themselves up to date with news of the world. However, it is their choice on what to be informed about. Many of which will use their phones daily to listen to music, get on social media, and keep up with celebrity gossip. Its okay to be up to date on these things however with the resource that is your cell phone to your disposal you should also be up to date on your culture's history, self help videos, current events (important issues, not always celebrity gossip/rumors), finance, and knowledge in general. You can literally learn how to do anything or get on the path to get started all with your phone.

Be respectful of your elders and be sure to listen to their stories and advice. Keep in mind that not all of Black history and the Black experience is on the internet or written in books.

Some of our elders have impactful stories from their personal lives that can be helpful for the youth although it is not public knowledge. Even if a elder is not a respectable person there's still something to be learned from them, even if they're an example of what you don't want to be like.

Although changing the negative thoughts elders have towards the younger generations is not your responsibility, the respect you show them and the willingness to learn and share knowledge with them may be the moment where you have changed their perceptions of the younger generations.

For The Older Generations-.

When older Black people have to think of the obstacles they had to endure and the promise they want for the future of Black people, it can be infuriating to deal with younger people who are concerned with nothing important. Although *some* may fall under the negative stereotypes concerning millennials not *all* of younger people are blissfully ignorant.

Some of the older generations would be surprised on how educated, well mannered, and ambitious some millennials and Generation Z youth are. The issue is that some of the older generations are judging younger people before knowing them or at least having a conversation with them.

Even if an elder meets a younger person who is not on the right path, many of our elders were lost in their youth as well. Not all of us were raised with the same resources or backing, so everyone will develop at their own pace. Given that Black people live in a world that oppresses them both historically and currently, the community must be patient with one another.

Never forget that Malcolm X was a criminal at a young age before he became the civil rights leader that he is known to be today. If we are honest with ourselves as a community, many younger people will grow up in single parent homes and are simply put living in a world not designed for them to win.

The community has to have some standards for living that the youth should abide by no doubt, however we have to give our youth time to grow. If you see someone younger than you on the wrong path, go and communicate the right way to them respectfully instead of criticizing them. Before judging a young person, try to remember how you were when you were young. Maybe you had a better hold on certain principles when you were young however I can guarantee that you made mistakes. You can look back on ways you could have been better. Everyone needs time to grow, will you be a helper or a criticizer?

Instead of harping on what the current generations are doing wrong, don't forget to acknowledge what they are doing right. Give compliments to the youth when you see them do the right things. Too often there's a spotlight on young people who confirm negative stereotypes about the younger generations while those who operate in a positive way can get overlooked or considered a rarity.

Whether you like it or not the youth have the future of the community in their hands. Show the youth the right way **RESPECTFULLY**. Be sure to applaud the youth when you see them do the right things and understand that you can learn great things from them. It's baffling how many elders demand respect but won't show it to the youth. You don't get something for nothing in this world, you have to give respect to get it.

Social stigmas and stereotypes concerning Black youth have vibrated into general social conscious so deep in the mind of the masses that a large population of Black people aim to look at black youth in a negative light until proven otherwise. in my younger years I would also observe many older people speak of Black youth in a negative way before knowing them. You will not be able to see the value of Black children and youth.

"The Black children are so disrespectful."

For the adults and parents reading this book, your job as a strong Black man or woman is to never give up on Black youth because they are our's and the future.

First, before you criticize any young person for character flaws, make sure you're an example of a person they should be like. Even if you are a person of high value, I'm sure you can look back at your younger years recalled times in which you could have done things better, or times in which you should have had a better attitude towards life. Always be patient with the youth, for as you (the adults reading this book) was granted time to learn and grow. The same opportunity should be extended to the youth. One may say, they are hard on the youth because they do not want younger people to fall for the same mistakes. This makes perfect sense but how you speak towards others means everything.

As often as possible be as kind and understanding as possible when dealing with the youth as they will deal with a world designed against them. Make sure they feel valued, accepted, and understood when you are in their presence.

All of us have emotional and character flaws we have to get over to be better people. You had your time of growth, so always be careful on being judgmental. No matter how troubled a generation is always make sure you are raising or assisting the youth in your family and around you in model fashion before you criticize any young person. Their will always be good and bad people of every generation, some of the elders tend to forget this.

Many elders and adults are nostalgic about their prime years coming up, however theirs many of which who can only recall the good memories but do not frame everything in its full perspective. For example an elder may say "In our day people stayed together, in long relationships! Nowadays people give up on relationships." Many would attribute this to the "lack of values" from the current generation. The elders who think in such a way fail to mention that some were actually stuck in relationships together. Women had less opportunities in the workplace and also women who had children from previous relationships were valued less.

This means that many women were stuck in abusive relationships, endured cheating and was expected to stay in the relationship. In short yes, couples of the past were more prone to stay together, but to say it is because of generational values alone, this would be false. Of course, such values cannot be completely ruled out, but an elder looking back may overlook all of the miserable relationship that were "stuck" together in the past.

When our elders only cherry pick all of the positive aspects of their generation, weighed against the full good and bad perspective of the youth, they are forming an unfair depiction of the youth, while being unfairly bias of their past. No generation is perfect, so stop acting like it.

We All Need Time To Grow -

Try to remember your youth once again. For me I had times where I got good grades, and times where I was barely passing. In my youth I talked respectfully, and at other times I cursed all the time (even so much that I got kicked off the bus in elementary school). I've made smart decisions and dumb ones just like everyone else. I fit in certain places and was the oddball in other places just like everyone else, I've succeeded and failed JUST LIKE EVERYONE ELSE. The difference between us is what do we learn and how we adapt to our own personal challenges.

Also try to understand an ignorant person can become a wise person in their own timing just as a person considered weak can become strong over time. Everyone will use their time going forward differently, some for the worst but also some for the better. Always make sure to view Black people in a positive light first. Understand that you may not like the way a young Black person is conducting themselves, but it is not fair to make snap judgments on who this person is if you don't know them personally.

Always be there for the young people and share the most important thing they need, your knowledge. Do your part and uplift the youth in any way you can instead of criticizing from a far. You should go the extra mile and be helpful and uplifting to children, teens, and young adults.

Judgement & Perception-

One of the most ignorant and arrogant things you can do is make a judgement of someone without knowing the full extent of who they are and what they have been through. Sometimes we can judge someone and be totally wrong in our judgement.

When I was young it was trendy for young Black men to wear their pants baggy, which lead to the sagging of pants. Understandingly many oppose this way of wearing clothes so much so that those who do it are easily judged. I'll admit that its disgusting to have your underwear showing, however what if a person who done such a thing grew up to be a major contributor to society? What if the person who sagged yesterday is a successful doctor, lawyer, or author today? The youth can be easily judged and ostracized in todays time; its as if our elders forgot that Malcolm X used to live the life of a career criminal before he became an icon.

Sometimes our own perception can get in the way of what reality is. I remember one time in my youth before I had my own car, I was getting picked up by friends to go to the mall. When my friends came, I rushed out the door to get in the car. It wasn't until I arrived at the mall that I realized I forgot to put on my belt! I wore baggy pants, but I did not like to sag, so I would normally wear pants what were sizes bigger than I should wear along with a belt to keep the pants on my hip. Since I did not have a belt, my pants were sagging as I walked through the mall. Do you think many elders gave me the benefit of the doubt? I'll answer that for you, hell no!

I was getting the "side eye" and disapproving looks from many everywhere I went. No one thought to give me the benefit of the doubt that I left my belt at home. Even till this day if I wear fitted pants with a fitted shirt I realize that sometimes I can sag on accident and not even realize it until I look down. I never liked sagging, however theirs been times where I have sagged, but that was not my intention. I can only image all of the snap judgments that were made of me because of the perception attached to sagging.

This is where we as a collective must practice giving each other the benefit of the doubt first. As people we can often make snap judgments before knowing the full story behind why someone does the things they do. When we assume the worst of each other first we play right in to the growth of Black oppression, when we see the best in each other we contribute to the growth of the Black community.

Community Service-

At a certain age of adulthood every Black person needs to find a way to give back to youth both inside and outside of their family. Every adult needs to be active in helping the youth be better prepared to succeed in this world in some sort of way or fashion. Black adults simply must pay it forward as soon as possible because of the hardships and issues those in elder generations had to endure. Making sure that younger people are better equipped than you were or assisting others who lack guidance is important. If you aren't helping the youth, you certainly don't deserve to talk bad about them because you aren't helping to shift the issue in the proper direction.

Correction-

The youth must be respected first before anything else. Just like any young person, Black youth are going to make mistakes, will get into trouble, and do stupid things. Of course corrections should take place because you should want to guide them in the best way possible.

When correcting a younger person always come from a "you can do better" standpoint instead of leading off with anger, scolding, and name calling. Some situations may be bigger than others. Always try your best to get a logical point by with sternness and not anger. Before you speak always keep in mind the times of your younger years when you have made mistakes, gotten into trouble, or have done stupid things.

Be intentional with your words. Know the difference between giving others constructive criticism and talking down to someone. Be relatable and understand where the youth are coming from and don't get caught up in always trying to lecture someone younger than you.

Be Receptive To Learning From The Youth:

One of the biggest reasons why some elders may not have respect for the youth is because they may not value their wisdom or feel like they can learn anything from them. One of my favorite authors John C. Maxwell had an perfect example of how you can learn a great deal from people you would least expect.

In the book *Winning With People* the author recalls a time when he went to a business conference. and when attending, wanted to skip the Q&A segment from small business owners in favor for speeches by the main guests; older, experienced, and successful businessmen. Out of curiosity Maxwell went to view the Q&A segment and recalled learning more from hearing his peers in the field speak, than when he listened to the experts later on that day.

Just like in this example, when we assume someone can't teach us something, we cut ourselves off from a great deal of information. As humans, we tend to have less respect for people we cannot learn from, which is why it's not ideal to think of the youth in such a fashion. If you are over 55 years old and reading this there's a possible chance that if you have children, they understand smart phones, computers, and the internet better than you. That's not to assume that some elders don't understand technology, but here we have an entire generation who will grow with technological devices far beyond thought possible maybe 30 years ago.

The elders and adults have knowledge of the past that can benefit you, the youth have the knowledge of the present which will always be important. Do not be fooled, the young have something valuable to teach us all if we are receptive. When the elders and adults realize they can learn from the youth, they will have no choice but to see them in a better view than the popular norm.

Root For The Young Black People-

Whether its young Black people in your family, in your community, or from a far, you should always want to see young Black people succeed. The youth should be encouraged and complimented when displaying their talents and abilities. The should always be told that they can be successful when they show talents or abilities. This is something that should apply to all young people of all races but especially is important for Black young people.

The Solution For Younger and Older Generations-

Many of the differences between youth and the elders can be solved by communicating and respecting each other. Some of the older generations see the youth as weaker because they endured more hardships than the younger generations, which creates barriers between the two groups.

As for our youth, imagine if you made sacrifices in your life to make conditions of people younger than you better and not only does the youth not know about it, but even worse, they don't care. Millennials, Generation-Z, and generations beyond, have to always realize that the elders had to make a lot of sacrifices for younger generations to live in a better world now. Your job as a young Black person is to know of the sacrifices that the older Black people had to endure.

Many millennials tend to allow the media or social media to tell them what's important. However, with cell phones and the internet you can decide what is important and worth looking up and knowing for yourself. Theirs no excuses anymore for being an ignorant person in 2023 and beyond.

Both older and younger generations can learn and grow from each other. Both have something to benefit not only each other but the entire Black community. Black people as a whole will grow and flourish when the younger and older generations, embrace, respect, and grow from each other.

- All generations of Black people need to
  - respect each other

- Understand that something valuable can be learned from all generations.

- Be receptive and listen to perspectives from people older and younger than you.

- Share your perspectives with people older and younger than you.

- Continually study history and keep up to date with current news.

- Do not look down on the youth before getting to know them.

- Be respectful to your elders and understand they have something you can learn from.

- People of all generations should not make assumptions about each other and should always strive to get to know each other on an individual basis.

- Give young people the benefit of the doubt, don't always assume they are up to no good.

- Speak to the youth in a respectful way, and remember to get respect, you must give respect.

- Contact the younger people in your family and check in with them like you would your parents and elders.

- If you are in close proximity to younger family members, make your presence known and show up for birthdays and attend as many events involving younger family members.

- Have someone younger than you teach you something new.

- Have young people who can keep you up to date on present day topics, technology, and ways of living.

- Give wisdom out of love and respect. Do not talk down to the youth so that you can feel superior.

WE WILL RESOLVE OUR ISSUES CONSTRUCTIVELY

One of the biggest problems facing the Black community is the lack of solving issues in a positive manner. This is the reason why Black individuals must have value in self so they can see value in others. Theirs some in the community who put many social ideologies on a higher level of importance than the racial bond they share with others in the community. Simply put theirs many Black people who value religions, political beliefs, occupations, money, place of origin, and current residency more than their Blackness or other Black people in general.

In many cases Black people have made each other enemies if they do not share the same ideologies. It is as if some have forgotten that they were born Black first before they became Christian or became Republican. It would be absurd to say all Black people put ideologies before their people but far too many are willing to resort to hostility and violence to resolve issues with each other. Some are not willing to at least have a conversation about the issues they may have with one another.

How can the Black dispora grow in totality if we are quick to harm one another? On another level it speaks to value of self. If you truly value the sacrifices the ancestors made would you be quick to harm another whom looks like you? I know you can think of people you don't like and people who don't like you. There's a good chance that if you and that person had an honest conversation, that you and the other person would most likely come to an understanding and at least respect one another.

It's understandable that some people have

attitudes and personalities that just wont tolerate one another, however even people who don't like one another can still respect or understand each other's point of view. Even if it has to come to harsh words with one another violence should be resorted to when it comes to self-defense only.

It is not implied that you should not defend yourself against anyone regardless of race, but it is implied that you take extreme haste to start an issue with another Black person especially. Black people collectively live in a world designed against them, theirs no benefit in conflict with each other. Be patient with one another and be slow to clash with each other. You can be sincere, stern, and honest, yet respectable in your tone. You should do everything in your power to avoid fighting.

Sure, one individual or a group of people can win a conflict, but usually where this one person or group wins, the community as a whole loses. When just 2 Black people resort to violence against each other, multiple communities suffer; 2 families suffer, and 2 lives could be ruined forever. Talk to each other about anything and everything. There is power in talking constructively about the problems you may have with one another, picking your battles, and sometimes just walking away from the situation.

Do not feel like you always have to prove to others that you are "hard" or you are "not soft." You may have too much to lose, and your best course of action may be to walk away from a negative situation all together.

Greeting Each Other in a Positive Way:

Theirs nothing wrong with being tough and having gumption, however theirs also nothing wrong with a man/woman reserving those attributes to only when they need to use them. Your toughness or attitude does not have to become your greeting towards people you don't know. The people who look like you and share similar life experiences on a macro scale should be the ones you should feel most comfortable around not the ones you should feel guarded around.

The Black community should feel comfortable around each other. Hard looks and tough posture is not how Black people should greet each other. Our men can smile, have fun, display a positive attitude, yet can become tough and hard when needed. We don't have to be soft men, but we don't have to be quick to violence against one another either.

Black women do not have to be in competition with each other or throw shade at another woman. They can see others who look like them as allies in the same fight. Ladies, always uplift each other and support each other. Black women come to the unique crossroads of dealing with racism (being Black) and gender issues (being a woman). No one on earth has to be stronger than Black women. This is why people of this unique group must be as supportive as possible around each other.

Black Family Conflict Resolution:

The Black family is an important factor in

the progress of the Black community. Dysfunction is normal in all family structures regardless of race. However Black people are living in a world designed against them. As said before *"we are not everyone else"* and do not have the same luxuries as other races do. We have no choice but to foster supportive families as we face issues that other races do not.

Too often members of Black families can become distant from one another over an issue that can be resolved over a simple conversation. If you cannot have difficult conversations, you will lose people and will not get what you truly want out of life. Children and teens are looking to their elders as an example of how they should act towards others.

Elders should respect the youth in the same way they want to be respected. If you are an older member of your family or a parent always keep in mind that the younger members in the family are watching and learning from you.

Your elders have life experiences that can help guide you through life, and possibly stop you from facing hardships they have faced. With each of them theirs knowledge of what one should do in life and what one should avoid. Be open minded and learn from the triumphs, failures, and knowledge that your elders are willing to share with you.

Allow for forgiveness and be willing to forgive as often as you can. Allow love to override the mistakes family members may make and reserve distance for those who threaten your safety and livelihood only. Keep in mind that Black people must build strong and loving families before they can foster strong and loving communities.

Black Relationships Conflict Resolution:

Disagreements happen in all relationships. How the two handle disagreements will be the difference between a good and bad relationship. Knowing how to effectively communicate and comprehend each other will contribute to the growth of the relationship. When there's a lack of considerate communication, the relationship suffers.

Black people need to love each other so much that they would never call each other out of their names just to get a point across. Simply discussing the facts in a respectful tone is all that is needed to make your point. Anything extra may cause things to get worse. Your partner should be able to be honest with you without having to deal with anger or negative attitudes.

If two people truly love each other name calling and physically hurting each other should never happen. If you have children together, these things should never happen in the household you all share. A child's parents are the first relationship they will see and will set the tone for how they want their relationships to be, or you could be an example of how they should not be in a relationship. Some will grow up to be exactly like their parents in relationships, while others will aspire to be different than their parents. No matter what your children choose to be, always be a positive role model for them.

All people of all races have to put a lot of

practice in to being positive, patient, and having a good attitude. Even though its more than understandable that Black people may be triggered to have negative attitudes more than people of other races because of racism and systematic oppression. As unfair as it seems, Black people must still rise above that and have a positive outlook.

If you and a significant other are having a disagreement talk to each other in a respectful manner while getting your point across. If tempers are too high, take some time apart to calm down. When the two of you are in a calmer state of mind you can talk about your issues without getting too emotional. If tempers are too high you may say things that are hurtful and do not resolve the issues you have. People in successful relationships do not aspire to win arguments or try to be "right." Instead they aspire to come to a resolution and an agreement that benefits both parties in the relationship.

Resolve Conflicts to Preserve Your Happiness:

Your happiness is your ancestors ultimate revenge. To find peace, love and happiness in a world designed against you is the highest form of success. Black people are doing an amazing job we just tend to not think so because we are easy to forget our past historic trauma along with a meager effort to right those past wrongs. The community can also have the tendency to compare their race to others races who have not faced the same measure of oppression. Black people have to remember that we are on our own timing and do not need to compare ourselves to other races, because others have not suffered in greater measure without being repaired.

Using statistics and examples to show the disparity in resources, income, and safety, as a means to display the racial inequality is understandable. However, Black people should not always try to use what people of other races have as a measuring stick. I once heard a phrase to the tune of "some Black people think White people's ice is cooler." Use the disparities in the racial gap as a statement to show the affects of systemic racism, but do not let it define your confidence. Always remember racism may make it harder for you to be successful but it can never stop you from being successful.

Make no mistake that many of issues affecting the Black community come at the hand of others and the US Government. The community must always battle against these forces while handling internal   issues. The root of many Black issues do not start within the Black community. As unfair as that may be, Black people must address what is in their immediate control; how they treat one another.

Hating, hurting, and killing one another strengthens our oppressions. Finding love and compassion for one another is one of the best things Black people can do. Look to resolve issues with one another and come to an understanding, do not look to win an argument or fight.

- When in disagreement with another seek a resolution and not conflict.

- Learn how to have respectful conversations about the issues you have with other people. Do not seek to be right or win the argument, instead seek to find a resolution both parties can agree on.

- Black strangers should greet each other in a positive way. No more hard looks when making eye contact with strangers who look like you.

- Family issues should be talked out in a kind and constructive manner. The goal should be to reach a resolution. Distancing from each other should only be used in extreme measures.

- Issues in Black relationships should be resolved with mature, respectful conversations. The goal isn't to dominate or win arguments. The couple wins when both parties can come to an agreement without attacking each other.

- Understand that part of being a responsible adult is having the ability to have difficult conversations without being too emotional.

- Remember that you are an example for the children who look up to you. They are learning from the way you handle disagreements.

WE WILL EDUCATE OURSELVES

The title of this law should be taken literally as in *"Educate Ourselves."* The problem with some people is they limit their intake of knowledge from what others tell them, or formal education from schools. Your knowledge may be limited if you only retain information that is told to you.

All Black people should seek more knowledge of their culture, history, self improvement, and community benefit. Whatever you would like to improve on in life there's a source of information that can help you in that area. Since we have smart phones and the internet their no excuse for not gaining access to information you need or desire.

Many people who own a phone will spend a great amount of time on social media, which is fine. However, the same device can be used to educate yourself on things that you will not learn in school. Some knowledge about Black history in totality is left out of formal education, and Black history is so broad that all that all of it cannot be condensed into a curriculum. Not to mention some information about Black history will be uncovered in recent time meaning it will not be covered in conventional text books or history books. You should aspire to learn something new about your people as much as possible.

Watching videos to laugh at and be entertained by is important yes, but watching motivational and self -help videos is just as if not more important than being entertained. We must be willing to know what information we need and how it will benefit us, if not we may become vulnerable to being only concerned with what the media or pop culture tells us is important.

Just as easy as it is for a Black person to name their top 5 favorite athletes and musicians, we should also be able to name our favorite civil rights leaders, historical figures, and business leaders. Seek beneficial information that will directly benefit your life instead of worrying so much about things that won't benefit you at all like celebrity gossip (unless you work in that field). Reading and studying self on a individual and cultural scale needs to be held in high importance in the Black community.

Leaving your education and the education of your children only in the hands of the public school system or formal education can be dangerous. Black people need to not only learn the formal lessons of a subject, but they also need to know about their history which is more broad than slavery, Jim Crow, and the Civil Rights Movement.

Leaning from as many Black educators in school and outside of school will be imperative to the growth and development of Black youth. Black educators and professionals can teach the technical side of a curriculum while also educating on how it is to be a Black person in their field of study and the unique circumstances that come from being Black in that field.

You can learn a great deal from someone outside your race, and actually it's a good practice to learn from other people and cultures.

Unfortunately people outside of your race may not be able to tell you what the Black experience is like. Learning from someone who shares the same race and culture as you can give you insight on what you may face in the real world.

I went to a predominately White university where such talks of a Black person's experience in the work place would come from the few Black professors on campus behind closed doors. For these reasons if a Black person were to choose to go to college, a historically black college may be a good option. Carter G. Woodson best explained it in his book *" The Mis-Education of the Negro":*

"The large majority of persons supposedly teaching Negros never carry to the schoolroom any thought as to improving their condition."

Leaving your learning just in the classrooms of a HBCU may be better for a black person, however it is always dangerous to leave your education in just a formal setting. Sadly, not every Black educator is for the development of their students. While some are, others are also just going through the motions until payday not caring the improve the lives of students.

Also I had a couple of White educators say words of encouragement and words of honesty I may not have heard anywhere else. These were people who had a purpose beyond a paycheck, however not every educator is going to be the same.

Even educators who have the best

intentions in mind can only teach you so much. They also have many other students to worry about. Leaving the depths of your education to one's curriculum can be detrimental. Even the best formal education in the best setting can only teach you so much. Your most profound lessons may be learned outside of the classroom.

Reading-

Going to the internet to look up information is a very good thing. However books contain in depth information that may not be available online. Read to learn the things you need to know or an area you want to learn and grow in. When you attend class in school you usually have a book that the class is referenced around. Be sure to do the same in your everyday life. When you discover your passion or area of interest invest in buying books that can take you to the next level.

You can read books that are autobiographies about successful people in your area of interest, informational books specific to your passion, and/or books that inspire you. Always have in your library books on motivation, self help, health, and success. Be sure to address areas that you need improvement in. Think of a book as a guide to help you navigate to where you are trying to go.

Also read books about general history and books about the history of your people. You must self educate and treat it as self maintenance like fitness, cleanliness, and nutrition. The worst thing you can do is leave the upkeep of yourself up to someone else. Reading books that entertain you is great, but reading books that motivate you and or help you grow are even better.

One advantage that information in books has over information online, is that books contain information that you would not know to look for. When you search for something online you must enter a key word to trigger the internet search for information. Books usually contain details that you may not think to look up, stories that you may not see online, perspectives you may not be able to find on the web.

One of the best books for Black people to buy and read *is Think And Grow Rich: A Black Choice* by Napoleon Hill and Dennis Kimbro. This book gives you motivation by way of success stories from Black people around the world and different time periods. Every Black household should have and read this book. *The Miseducation of the Negro* by Carter G. Woodson, and *Powernomics* by Claude Anderson is also a must have in Black households. Theirs plenty of other books you should read. Make reading a lifelong endeavor as theirs always more to know and more perspectives to consider. No matter how much you know, there's always more to learn. Formal education will never teach you enough about the experience of Black people.

You want to always be prepared to live in a world without electricity, so make sure you have resources, guides, and knowledge other than digital references. This is not to degrade using online sources and materials for knowledge and growth, its just that in 2023 one may only rely on digital sources for learning, growth, and knowledge, which can be of detriment to the person if digital sources are no longer available. Its always good to have tangible sources for learning like books and magazines along with using online sources.

Learning on the internet-

In 2023 we use the internet for almost everything. It's baffling if you are not using it to educate or better yourself. The good thing about the internet is that you get uncensored information from multiple sources, and it is easier than ever to seek information in its rawest form.

In today's world you will spend more time on your phone than watching TV. You perhaps may spend more time looking at your phone than driving. If you are going to devote so much time to your device at least spend some of that time on something that will benefit you. Learn something new every day in your field of interest or general self development. If you look up enough good self development videos on YouTube, the algorithm will send more videos related to the topic in your "recommended" videos.

There's a vast amount of information online and in videos on topics that may not be in the books you have on hand. Also, you can look up such information at any time, any place. I often watch videos of ancient African kings, queen, and empires. You can also look up areas of interest surrounding your culture. For instance, since I'm an artist I may look up "Prominent Black artist", and it will bring up videos of successful Black artist that I've never heard of in school.

One can look up videos of Black excellence in any period of time. Always keep in mind however that most videos are a condensed summary of what happened historically. When it comes to a craft, videos online can only give you so much knowledge. Some videos may be long and in depth, however most details will be in books about the subject. Don't limit yourself to only reading books or only surfing the internet for information. Make sure you are using both methods to learn and grow.

Experience of the Elders:

Most older people have experiences we either want for ourselves and/or experiences we don't want to go through. The elders may have a firsthand experience on history so they are worth listening to. From older people you can find examples of who you would like to be and some examples of who you do not want to be.

Some of the things we need to learn about aren't in books or are not covered in someone's video. Some of the best knowledge is gained by word of mouth.. Just like with any source of information always check the facts of what someone tells you as some people lie or embellish the truth.

Be open minded and respectfully listen when someone has a helpful word, as the words that may impact you the most may come from the people you least expect. Some people may come into your life just to deliver a message or lesson you need and nothing more. Honor the effort an elder takes to share knowledge with you, as they do not have to take the time to share these lessons with you.

Some elders know the past issues that we currently live with today. They can be a resource to help solve the issues that we currently deal with. The elders also have knowledge from the past that may not be seen as valuable in today's time but is still useful nonetheless. The elders may have the knowledge that you cannot find online. Learn the skills that the elders have so you can be more self-reliant and not solely dependent on others or technology. Some elders may teach you things that your parents cannot, so always be open minded and at least listen to what the elders have to say.

Experience of the Youth:

Sometimes elders may think theirs nothing the youth can teach them because they are older thus wiser, know more, and have more experiences in life. The youth may have less experiences in life, however they may have current perspectives of the present and future that the elders may not know of or have a perspective on.

The youth can help some elders understand the changing world around them. The youth also understand technology and shifts in society that older people may not understand. They can also shed light on modern issues that Black people deal with that the older age groups may not be aware of.

New perspectives on life and certain subjects may disprove older ways of thinking or older perspectives that the elders may hold on to. If you think you cannot learn from the youth, then you think of the last time you had an issue with your cell phone. If you cannot reach the company for assistance or talk to a tech expert, I'm more than sure a young person in your family could solve the issue. Technology is constantly evolving and children growing up with these technological advancements on average will understand it better than their elders, sometimes even their parents.

Whether old or young everyone has knowledge that is valuable to someone. The youth and elders both have insight and perspectives that will prove valuable to each other. Elders, do not let generational bias and stereotypes convince you that theirs no value to the current or younger generations. The youth have something to teach you, if you are not willing to learn from them, you will be lost in time.

Self Refection:

When you gather information from any source it's always reported by someone else or from the perspective of someone else. An important question to ask yourself is "what do I think?" or "what's my perspective on this issue?" Gathering your own perspective or opinion on a topic instead of just always going along with the word of others can do wonders for your analytic skills.

Sometimes it's good to come to your own conclusion on an issue instead of feeling like you must always side with what someone else is thinking. Think deeply about issues and think of the solutions you can come up with. It's even healthy to gather opinions on topics and issues in your head or to yourself if you don't have anyone to discuss issues of interest with. Forming opinions for yourself is one of the best ways to encourage you to think for yourself and look for your own perspectives on issues.

Some answers will come to us during deep reflection on issues in our own mind. While you have to learn externally to find information on historical facts, dates, and specific information, you can learn internally by way of your own perspective, forming your own principles, and coming up with a lifestyle that best suits you.

Learning yourself also allows you to realize what you are good at and what you need to improve on personally, if you can be honest with yourself. Knowing what you have to offer and what you need to improve on will be valuable for a lifetime. You cannot learn everything on your own, but knowing yourself is one of the most valuable things you can do.

My Experience:

I have learned a good amount of Black

history in high school and college but of course it was information starting with Black slavery and the overcoming of that oppression. Since the subject is so broad, I realized I could only learn a few limited things from a school curriculum. For me, I retained stories of courage, endurance, and persistence within our struggle to be equals in America. While I see it one way, another may see our American history as an oppressed, hopeless people, with no way of being equal to a dominate class.

I personally know of many younger Black people who are oblivious to their history and even worse, they don't care to know. In my opinion most Black people who know a fuller sense of Black history, seem to embrace, and have a deeper love for Black people and the Black community. Educating yourself more about who you are and who you can be will help you see other Black people in a proper sight.

I learned most of the important things about Black history outside of a traditional classroom. This is why you must be willing to learn about Black history and culture on your own, to discover the details that formal education will not teach you.

When Black people learn about themselves in depth, it allows them to become a teacher of self. You will be empowered to come up with your own conclusion on things and not just to follow what someone else says. When you seek education for yourself you can become the teacher and the student. You will also be able to teach others and inform them about things they should know.

How you choose to learn is completely up to you. What's most important is that you have a thirst for knowledge. Every Black person should want to know their people's own history/culture, health practices, finance management, mental health management, and whatever job or task they want to take on in life.

Theirs a population of Black people who doubt their abilities to be intelligent. They give in to what "statistics" and what is popularly held as a belief that they naturally struggle in areas of learning when it comes to math and science. Rapper/ Activist David Banner and Activist/ Author Claude Anderson echoed the same sentiments of the power of Black intelligence never seen before. Before a Black person doubts their learning abilities remember what both Claude Anderson and David Banner said, from 1800-1865 90% of Black people could not read or write as it was made illegal for them to do so. After slavery, illiteracy was reduced to an astounding 42% within just 30 years, no other race on earth has done this. Believe in the power of your intelligence.

- Actively learn something new about self-improvement once a week.

- Learn something new about your craft at least once a week.

- Continuously read books. Set aside daily time for reading.

- Learn of a Black leader you were unaware of.

- Subscribe to YouTube channels and blog sites related to information that is important to your health, finances, history, and field of interest.

- Get at least 1 new book a month.

- Be a respectful ear to elders. Do not take their knowledge for granted

- Be a source of knowledge for people younger than you.

- Realize that you can learn from those who are younger than you. Do not underestimate the knowledge of the youth.

- Be a lover of knowledge. Learn from books, articles, videos, and the wisdom of others.

- Follow social media accounts and subscribe to accounts that help you learn in the areas of health, history, and self-development.

WE WILL VALUE THE OPPOSITE GENDER

The stigma of Black people worldwide has caused many in the community to take on negative beliefs and views of the opposite gender. From a general stereotypical standpoint, Black women can be thought of as being emotionally unstable, having horrible attitudes, ghetto, and thought of to be less desirable compared to women of other races. On the other end Black men are thought of as being poor, financially uneducated, criminals, ghetto influenced, poorly educated, immature, and/or thought of as poor leaders and providers.

Once again, we may not control the narrative the world has for us, but that does not mean we have to accept and embrace it. Theirs plenty of Black people both female and male who are nothing like the negative stereotypes associated with the community. However it is common human nature to believe the narrative more than reality. Black people can believe and embraces their own ideas of what our women and men are and what they represent.

How Black Women Should Be Treated

All humans originated from Black women, therefore they should be thought of with high regard by everyone. From a historical standpoint, Black women have been on the front lines of every movement to advance the lives of Black people and others. Some Black men cherish Black women (thank you for that), however we will speak to those who don't. Some men think of Black women as *bitches* and *hoes* until shown otherwise. Are all women worthy of praise? No, however a woman should not be looked down on until proved otherwise. Instead Black women should be seen a queens first until proven otherwise.

As a collective Black men need to protect and celebrate Black women, especially in today's time. As a group, Black women may be doing better than they ever have. Recently (2024) Black women are becoming entrepreneurs at a higher rate than any other minority group, which is something all Black people should be proud of. Cora Daniels stated in *Black Power Inc.* :

"According to the Center for Women's Business Research, 36 percent of Black women said they became entrepreneurs after hitting the glass ceiling."

She goes on to say that this is just one of many instances where Black women use their discrimination as motivation and are "turning to action" instead of just accepting what the corporate world offers them. These brave women need to be loved, supported, and protected at all times. Black men should treat the women in their family with respect, and they should treat women outside of their family in the same fashion.

No one on earth has had to be stronger and more enduring than the Black woman. Being strong however takes a toll on anyone. You need someone to love you and care for you when you have to be strong for the world. No one can relate to what Black women have to deal with, which is why they should always feel supported by Black men.

How Black Men Should Be Treated

The Black man is one of the most disrespected group of people on the planet. The same scorn should not come from Black women. Black men should NOT be generalized by Black women due to worldly stereotypes: being unfaithful, unreliable, and immature. A Black man should not be devalued before getting to know him. Too often men of all races are generalized as being and thinking the same, and it seems to be doubly true for Black men.

If Black men have to deal with constant stigma from the world we all live in, then it's the Black woman's job to be supportive, encouraging, and loving. He should be respected first, before being assumed to be what generalizations and stereotypes make him out to be, until at least proven otherwise.

Both Black women and men will meet people who are the living embodiment of all the negative associations mentioned before. Yet and still it is up to members of the community to make sure that the few "bad" people that we meet don't become the association for the entire gender. For the most part, people of other races tend to associate negative characteristics with the individual, not the entire group. Black men and women must do the same and not let a few individuals be the spokesperson for an entire race and gender.

Black men may be underestimated by many others in world but they should never be thought of in such a way by Black women. Naturally men are thought of as the leaders in a society. We know this not be true in reality, but from a cultural standpoint, devaluing the men of a race allows justification for others to control a race. When the value of a group of people are thought of in a low spectrum, any negative example from a single member, is thought to represent the whole. Let us ask, is this fair? No!

When people of other races commit crimes or do negative things for the most part they are individualized, yet in the Black community, these negative few represent the whole. For example if one Black person shows up late for an event, it is "normal" because they are on "colored people time." When I do events clients who are Black normalize such thoughts and even jokingly say "you know how we do, we are never on time." Yet showing up on time is not racial issue but a human issue. It may surprise some of my Black customers to learn that my White, Asian, and Hispanic customers ALSO struggle with punctuality; their events don't start on time every time either. Yet I never hear a White or Hispanic person make the claim that its culturally normal for member of the race to show up late. They usually say it's the individual person who is late not make it a racial aspect.

I feel the same sentiments being a Black man, where most of the negative stereotypes associated with the race are thought of to be true. The actions of individuals seem to represent the whole. Too many Black women have a long list of negative associations when it comes to Black men long before they think of positive aspects. I know that some Black women have been in bad relationships with Black men, but what our people need to realize is that theirs relationship issues among all races. All humans at some point of or another struggle with relationships concerning the opposite sex.

Even those who are in happy relationships now, can most likely think of a time where they have had difficulty in a relationship with someone else. I know of many happy Black couples and marriages, but the norm is that Black men and women struggle in relationships with each other. Even in the Black community too often the negative associations are always thought of to be true even if theirs exceptions right in front of us.

Every Black man deserves a chance to prove who he is before attaching the world's negative image on him. Others may generalize Black men, but Black women must continue to be our back bone and the loving person of refuge that we can confide in. We are in a fight together so we have to love each other.

Interracial Relationships:

"That sounds good, but I'm in love with someone outside of my race."

Love can be a tough emotion to understand. In a sometimes cruel world we live in, its normal for us as people in general to hold on and be with people who are there for us and love us unconditionally whether Black or any other race.

Some of the most amazing Black people have come from interracial relationships where one of the parents are non-Black. Since someone who loves you is usually there through thick and thin, it is impossible to tell people who they should love. Of course, Black love and Black unions are encouraged to help build and keep the community strong, however sometimes one cannot help who they love.

We all have different reasons for loving who we love, which may not be apparent to those outside of the relationship. An interracial relationship becomes an issue when people of other races are thought of to be better than their own and being the main reason for choosing a partner outside of your race. To have a preference of someone non-Black because you think they are better because of race is absolutely wrong.

Theirs good and bad people of all races, so to disrespect Black people solely due to a few bad personal experiences, generalizations, and stereotypes is unfair. Wise people know there's always exceptions and people who live outside of negative stereotypes. No matter how many Black men or women you have dated and ended on a bad note, theirs still millions of good Black people worth dating globally.

Is it fair to be dismissive of your own people over a few limited experiences you've had? For example, if you were in 5 bad relationships with Black people is it fair to blame an entire race for such results? 5 people is not even a fraction of the available and loving Black people of this world. Not to mention as of 2024 divorce rates are higher among interracial marriages than same race marriages. This is not to say interracial marriages don't work; however it proves that simply just jumping to a different race may not make your relationship woes go away.

We also have to keep in mind that relationships are always a two-way street where both parties bare some responsibility for how the relationship turns out (some more than others). A wise person always looks at the part they themselves have played in the success or failure of the relationship.

Remember, even if you end up with someone outside of your race, theirs still a possibility your children will be identified as Black by the rest of society. Even if your offspring is technically multi racial, they may take on the ideology of Blackness regardless of having a non-Black parent. This person may also find difficulty fitting in with the other race they are part of because of their Blackness.

This is why it's imperative that if you do decide to be with someone non-Black they must understand the issues facing the community and be supportive for the advancement of Black people. Understand that just because someone loves you or engages in physical relationships with you does not mean they have love and support for the entire Black community. The person has to be able to raise a person who will be half Black whom of which will have to deal with a world in which they may be oppressed for the Blackness they have. Advancements for Black people is also advancements for their child as well. Before you commit to anyone, make sure they support the advancement of your people.

- Black men should be gentlemen to all women, but especially to Black women meaning; opening doors, being polite, having manners, not talking over them when they are trying to speak, and giving them assistance while doing manual labor task.

- Examine your past relationships. Find where YOU were wrong or the negative one. Forgive yourself and make sure you do not repeat the same mistakes.

- Allow for new people you date to start with a new slate. Learn from old relationships, but do not carry baggage from old relationships into new relationships.

- Allow for teachable moments in relationships. Not everyone is equipped with the knowledge you have.

- Learn from relationships that do not work out, do not become jaded by them.

- Do not engage in talks with others who try to degrade the opposite gender of Black people

- Do not be afraid to defend the opposite gender of the Black race when others try to degrade the opposite gender.

- Have unlimited love for the race you belong to no matter how many individuals do you wrong.

WE WILL HAVE A STRONG FAMILY UNITY

Black people need to form strong family units in order to form strong communities. We should be supportive and uplifting of each other on all accounts. Black families should affirm and believe in the best of each other until proven otherwise. If one needs correction it should be with love in mind and keeping strong relationships. Points can be made sternly without name calling, embarrassment and verbal abuse. When differences are tough to solve, loving each other must be paramount. A family member should be a person you are willing to have the most forgiveness for excluding extreme circumstances.

"Families of other races aren't all perfect either"

It is true that families of many other ethnic backgrounds are dysfunctional which has given many the idea of a divided family as normal. Black Americans must realize you are the only race of people to survive the type of oppression historically without being rewarded proper reparations. Black families should act like it. Act as if you need to depend on each other more than the rest of the world. Due to the historic oppression endured by Black ancestors and the transformed current day racial issues, Black people do not have the luxury to have dysfunctional families.

Younger family members should always be molded in the right way and helped out in any way possible. Black children should be raised in a family community function not from just an immediate family standpoint. The youth should always know who has their back and who will support them. Uncles and aunts should be active in the raising, nurturing, and protecting of their nieces and nephews.

Youth In Your Family-

The community should want and aspire for the youth that come after them to have better opportunities and better positioned to be successful in life. Collectively we should always aspire to show the youth good principles of living and the right character it takes to be successful. Elders should not want the youth to experience the same strife and struggles that they suffered.

Whatever the youth in your family plans to do they should have the full support of the family as long as its morally ethical. When a young family member is wrong or going through hardship, it is the family's role to be supportive and aiding in correction not to criticize and gossip about them. Always make sure the youth in your family knows that you are there for them and you believe in them.

When birthdays, holidays, celebrations, and special occasions happen for the young people in the family as many elders as possible should come together and pitch in equally for a celebration. Putting celebrations on the shoulders of one person should never happen. The family should come together as a group to bring events and celebrations to life. Black children and youth will grow up with judgment from their peers, teachers, and society as a whole. Always make sure they know that their family has their back and loves them.

Be Good Children For Your Parents-

As children we must always remember that

our parents had to make sacrifices that we couldn't imagine just for us to live normal lives. Some of our parents even had to put their wants, ambitions, and dreams aside if not give them up all together just to provide a better life for their children.

Given that technically none of us asked to be here, it is still a great privilege to have great parents because not everyone is blessed with such. Just as your parents have been in services to you much of your life, you owe it to them to be a service to them as soon as possible. Your parents may have worked jobs they have hated and deal with situations they did not want to be in just to provide for you.

Serving Your Parent in Childhood-

While you're young your parents may be in service to you and expect nothing in return. If you have good nurturing parents, they will take care of you because they love you not because they want something in return. If you truly love your parents and appreciate the sacrifices they have made, you should be in service to them whether they ask for it or not.

If you are a young child reading this book, you should get good grades in school, but do more than that. You should make sure the house is clean without parents asking you to do so. If you are of age, you should also take the time to cook for them as well. Most likely your parent(s) are working hard to pay bills that you can't afford to pay, along with getting the things you want but can't afford on your own. Make sure you are contributing to the household in some sort or fashion.

Your parents may delegate task to you, if they don't ask them how you can be more helpful around the house. If you are older reading this book and this time has past the both of you, make sure you at the very least tell your parents thank you for providing a way for you to live your life. Do not take good parent for granted, make sure at the very least, they always feel appreciated. Always ask how you can be of service to them.

Serving Your Parent As A Teen/ Young Adult-

If you are still in high school your most important goal is getting good grades. Getting good grades does not guarantee anything, however one thing it can do for you is give you more options as to what you want to do in your future. This is the least you can do for your parents. The worst thing ever is breaking you back on the job and providing a way for your children while they are not even trying to apply themselves in school.

Most likely your parents will delegate task and choirs to you. To show your appreciation do these task with enthusiasm and make sure they do not have to constantly remind you to do so. If you are a student-athlete give your all in the sport you are in to make you parents proud. Your parents have to invest in your athletic career and some of which make time to see you do this sport on top of an already busy schedule. Make sure you play to the best of your abilities and perform in a way that would make them proud. Give your best effort and you may be able to get a scholarship to improve the life of you and your parents.

Make sure every birthday you do something for your parents to show you that you love them. You don't have to wait for these days to do something special for your parents, however you should make sure to do something for them on those days. Do everything in a manner that would make your parents proud. You can never say "thank you" too much to your parents; make them feel appreciated as much as possible.

Serving Your Parent As Adults-

The ultimate thank you is taking care of your parents in as many ways as you can when they get older. This means making sure they have a good quality of life in their older years. Your goal should be to make sure your parents are mentally, physically, and financially taken care of as they grow older. Even if they don't ask, you should aspire to care for them in as many ways as possible.

As much as you want to be successful for yourself, your children, and your significant other, you should aspire to be successful to benefit your parents as well. If your parents have everything they need in place ask them what they need done.

If they don't need or want anything from you, you should aim to spoil them anyways. You need to make sure they know you appreciate what they have done for you during the majority of your life. You want to make sure your parents are set up for retirement and that their mental and o do the same thing or make sure others can do the task of caring for them as they get older.

Elders In The Family-

More often than not the elders in the family experienced hardships in the past that we may not endure, which means they should be respected first until shown otherwise. An elder's wisdom should never be taken for granted and although you may not agree with everything they say, they at least deserve to be listened to by the youth. Theirs a lesson in the stories and wisdom of all elders regardless of what social status they have.

Elders should be checked on regularly and made sure that you are willing to assist them in any way possible. Just as the elders make sacrifices to raise the youth, the youth should make sure the lives of the elders are made easier so that the sacrifices made by elders were not made in vain.

Be sure to call your older family members and check on them at least on a (weekly basis). Visit them from time to time and ask a question; "Can I help you with anything?" The reason why you must ask your elders this question is that usually as people we will tell others we are "fine" even when they aren't. Visiting them can give you an accurate account of how they are truly doing. Talk to them in person as much as possible to get a good feel for how they are doing.

The Nurturing Parent-

If Black men and woman can't foster good relationships they cannot build strong families and if we cannot build strong families we cannot build strong communities. In an ideal situation it would be best if parents stay in loving relationship with each other and raise the children they had with each other. It's a good idea to have children with people you can have long term relationships with, however in real life, love and relationships can be more complicated than what we would want them to be.

Sometimes it just won't work out with the person you have had a child with. Although in perfect world we would wish that circumstances would be different, however in the real world it just won't work out even with the best of intentions. No matter how you feel about the person you have had a child with, it is the duty of the both of you to take care of and nurture the child you have had together.

Married With Children-

Being and staying together while raising a child or children is the ideal situation to be in. Your sons/daughters will benefit a great amount by seeing their parent in a loving relationship. They should learn important lifelong lessons from a male and female perspective by the people who care for them the most. Nothing is better than having your mother and father in the same house as a resource on how to live a righteous life.

Having both parents in the house hold doesn't guarantee that child will benefit all the ways they need to be a full functioning adult, but both parents do give a child the best odds the grow with the tools they need to be a successful adults. Seeing both parents keep and maintain a good relationship gives them the best odds to do the same when they become adults. A strong loving family unit is very beneficial to the Black community as not only an example for others but the offspring will reap more benefits having both parents in the household.

Co-Parenting-

I believe as Black people perhaps we should be more selective with the partners we not only date but choose to have sex with. As a young man my mom told me to select quality over quantity. Of course many of my peers would say otherwise but I chose to listen to my mothers wise words, she would go on to say "every person you have sex with could potentially be the mother of your child."

Black people should try at every end to stay with the person they are going to bring a child in this world with. In the book **Black Fatherhood The Guide To Male Parenting by Earl Hutchinson**, one of the many fathers said the following:

" *If a black man and woman could deal*

*with each other when things were bad, then
they can deal with each other now that things
are relatively better and they have choices."*

In this quote lies the double edge sword
that is the modern Black relationship. Although
many things are easier for Black people in
present times, the same issue is that we don't
have to rely on each other as much as we did
when times were harder. Granted in the past
women had less options in society and found
themselves with less options without a man in
the household.

If the Black community can find a way to
cultivate and keep more meaningful
relationships it will benefit all parties involved.
Although divorce rates are high than the past
among all races keep in mind that no one has
suffered more oppression than Black people, so
Black children facing this world need both
parents or two parents in the household more
than any other race.

Sometimes you can give your best effort
towards the relationship and although you tried
your best it just won't work out. Even though
the relationship has failed that doesn't mean
you have to fail as parents. Theirs many factors
that come into play as to why a relationship will
not work out, but theirs no excuse to fail as
parents.

If you bring a child in this world both
mother and father share responsibility to do
whatever you can to best equip the child. For
the women this means no using your children
as bait to do what you want to the father of the
child. And for the father just because the

mother has custody of the child does not mean you get to abandon your responsibilities as a father. This means more than just being an ATM and throwing money at the situation. You have to put in effort to help raise the child. If you and the mother stay in the same city and state this means seeing your child and giving them the life long lesson and attention they need.

I was glad to see one of my good friends call his son, he told me he does so at least once a week if not everyday if he can. If you live in a different state than the mother of the child who has custody, you should do the same. Both mother and father must raise beyond being bitter that the relationship did not work out and put the needs of the child first.

Single Parents-

Some parents are in the unfortunate situation where the other parent has completely abandoned responsibility of doing their part in raising the child, or even worse has passed away. Being A single parent is a challenging ordeal that may not seem fair, however it can be successfully done. When you bring a significant other around your children you need to make sure they respect and can foster love for your child.

It may be hard not to be bitter about the situation you are in whether you are a single mom or a single dad where the other parent is absent. It's not fair that you have to take on the burden of both parents, but if you must do so, you should want better circumstances for your children. Make sure you aren't resentful of the opposite gender and teach such things to your children.

Your child can learn fatherly or motherly lessons from other people in your family or other people that they look up to whether they are famous people or people they know personally. If the other parent wants to be apart of the child's life, do not cut them off from their child because the relationship did not work out. Always keep in mind that you must do what is in the best interest of the child. In fact it is even ideal to make sure that the other parent of the child is in good standing, not for your sake but for the child's sake.

Participate In Your Child's Education:

In this book I ask you to seek education outside of what you would learn in formal education. In the book *Black Fatherhood* the same is asked of its readers but even goes a step further and gives a plan of action. Not only should you teach your children outside of school, you should be active in their education while in school.

The book suggest that Black fathers can come together to form committees that work with teachers, plan activities, volunteer to be classroom assistants, tutors, and attend PTA meetings. Most importantly the book asks the committee of Black fathers to advise the school administration on policies, programs, and philosophies geared towards Black children. It also states that these band of Black fathers should voice concerns at school board meeting.

Of course Black mothers can and should do the same. Black parents should be very strategic when it comes to the education of their children.

Keep The Balance:

I'm a new father, so it would be wrong of me to tell someone how to raise their children. Every parent has their own parenting style, some may be more easy going while others may be more stern. I'd say instead of playing either end of the spectrum be situational and adapt to the situation. In some situations its good to be easy going, in other situations it's better to be stern, being a good parent is knowing when to be which.

Some disagree with the notion of being a "friend" to your children. Although you may feel the need to maintain an authoritative stance in the relationship with your child, but understand, being too authoritative, or stern may cause your children to rebel against you. They may sneak behind your back to do things. If you are too hard on your children, they can become bullies. The opposite affect can happen, and they can become timid and not stand up for themselves too. If you can't relate to them and allow them to open up to you freely, they may keep things hidden from you and ask their peers for advice instead of you.

If you are too easy going with your children and do not set boundaries and responsibilities it can also work against them. Irresponsible children can easily turn into irresponsible adults. Don't think about how you were treated as a child, think about how you would like to have been treated as a child, and act in that fashion towards your children. Being too stern can not only be stressful on your children, but stressful on you as well.

Take Care Of Yourself:

When you have children, most of the time your wants get put on the back burner for the child's needs. It can seem like your life can be consumed with taking care of your children. You have to find time to yourself to take care of yourself, so you can be helpful to everyone else. You are no good to your family when you are burnt out and stressed.

You have to take time to relax and enjoy life. Find something that you like to do or you find fun at least once a week. Your household will absorb your energy, so it is important to maintain a positive and happy mindset when in the household as much as possible. Assess where you are mentally and address what you need to do to relax.

When we don't find pleasure in life, we can become resentful of the same things that are supposed to motivate us, because the lack of happiness makes us feel like slaves to these things. We all know of that one parent who has a horrible attitude towards their own children. They are short tempered with them, quick to humiliate them, and/or would prefer not to be bothered by them at all.

One could say it is because the stress they feel on the job which makes them feel drained. One could say that some parents resent their children because they feel like their children are

143

the reason why they live a life full of stress and mounting responsibilities. If you have children, do not let this be you. Finding time for yourself is not a selfish thing, and it is what's best for you, your children, and the household.

Family Business-

Keeping the money in the family sounds like a good practice but, making money in the family sounds even better. Whether it's a family operated business, or family members investing in a family member already established business is a practice worth trying. Having a business among family members and creating a source of income for members involved can substantially secure income for Black people whether than being dependent on the job market. Making sure family members get paid is also benefiting your nieces, nephews, and second cousins of the family. Just like any other business theirs no guarantees that a family business idea will work out but its definitely worth trying for all the benefits that could come from creating a successful vehicle of income.

A family business will allow for collectively making money, saving and allowing for business ideas to be moved on faster and easier if done collectively. Saved money can be invested into a family trust, emergency accounts, family events, stocks, investments into outside businesses, and the purchase of property and land. Theirs no limit to the businesses family members can do together. This will allow for Black family members to generate income on their own power and less reliant to what's available on the job market.

In this life if you want to run a business you want to make it as easy for yourself as possible. Finding man power, capitol, loans, and partners will be easier accessed among family members than others if a family business can be ran effectively. It will be key for family members in business together to be able to keep business and personal relationships separate. No matter what happens in business love for each other must remain whether failure or success.

Family members do not need to have a lot of money to invest in business ideas, as just $20 just among 5 family members is $100 towards any cause of the business. Small investments like $20 from multiple family members can add up and it is an investment amount that anyone could afford.

Look inward for your strength instead of outward. Look at yourself and figure out what you have to offer or a good business idea that you and others in the family could profit from. Try to pinpoint people in your family who would be good to go in business with or have something to offer of entrepreneurial value. Having income among your family will give you more mobility and liberty in life.

Having better control of income can empower a Black person to have more time to dedicate to parenting or other things of interest. Even if you don't want to be fully emerged in a business you could take part by passively investing money, time, or resources into business. Investing in a family business is a good idea because it allows for a possible back up plan or something to fall back on if things don't work out in your job or career.

Support-

Family should travel together, bond together, and support each other's endeavors. The young members of the family should have many family members at their events while growing up. Family members may not fit in with certain places in society, but they should always feel secure when around each other. I can guarantee their will be disagreements, arguments, and even fights in your family. Always look for resolutions to all disagreements. If it does not involve health, safety, and livelihood of family members, most issue can and should be resolved.

- Communicated at with younger and elder family members at least once a month

- When one has birthdays and celebrations, family members should participate by being apart of the celebration and helping put it together.

- Contact family members you have issues with and have a honest yet respectful conversation and see if the two of you can come to an agreement.

- Attend as many events that your family members have.

- If your family members are entrepreneurs support their business by buying their products and promoting their business to others.

- Make it a priority to discuss business and income opportunities as a family.

- Do NOT engage in gossip talk or derogatory comments about family members.

- When having issues or problems, talk about the situations and allow the other person to explain their side of the story. Try to see their point of view and perception. Be slow to anger and avoid arguing and fighting. Figure out issues to find a resolution, not to win an argument.

- If you don't have children, be very mindful of the person you choose to have children with. Think of people you would have long term meaningful relationships to have children with.

- Do your best to maintain your family unit, its one of the most important things you can do in life.

- Maintain a good, balanced relationship with your children or the young people in your life. Understand when its the right time to be stern and when you can take it easy.

- If you are co-parenting, put the needs of the child first. If past issues cannot be resolved at least get on a cordial relationship with the other parent for the sake of the child. At least be able to communicate good enough to where you can both effectively care of the children.

- Make sure you think of your children as your motivation and not as your bondage.

- Make some time for yourself and do at least 1 relaxing activity and 1 activity you enjoy at least once a week.

- Keep peaceful, happy, loving, and positive energy in the household as much as possible.

- Have a family reunion at least once a year.

- Make sure the youth and elders are both equally valued.

- Call your parent /guardian today and tell them "Thank you" for all they have done for you.

- Make sure your parents are acknowledged in some way during the holidays, but also pick some random days throughout the year to show your parents you appreciate them.

- Assess how you were raised and copy the things your parent did that was beneficial to you, change the ways that had a negative effect on you.

- Call your parents as much as
  possible. No matter what happens
  in life, one day you won't be able to.

- Try to physically see your parents
  as much as possible. The older they
  are, make it a point to see them as
  often as possible.

- Live a life that your parent would
  be proud of. This does not mean
  you will do as your parents want
  you to do career wise or living wise,
  but make sure you do your craft to
  the best of your abilities. Chase
  your goals, take care of your
  responsibilities, be healthy, and be
  happy.

WE WILL BE SMART WITH OUR MONEY

According to stereotypes and probably any statistical charts out there, Black people are thought of as being financially irresponsible. To handle finances properly most people in this world have to put off "keeping up with the Jones's" or "stunt culture". This means spending on necessities first, saving for short term/ long term emergencies, saving for investments, and then at last you can spend on what you want.

Carter G. Woodson described in his book *"The Mis-Education of the Negro"* how a woman came to him looking for financial help all while wearing a jacket that cost enough to get her out of the problems she had. Too many Black people have the mindset of **looking** secure instead of **being** secure. Theirs been many times when I would hear someone complain about finances with $200 shoes on their feet. Or a family facing foreclosure on their home with a Mercedes in the driveway. The very money that some of spend on clothes, cars, and liabilities which make them look rich or secure to others, could be used in a more beneficial way, so that one day they can actually afford what they want.

Being fiscally responsible can help put you and your family in a better position instead of looking the part or being too ignorant to know what to do with your money. Saving money isn't always easy but it is a necessity. Treat saving money like a bill that you will owe to yourself in the future. This also means being smart in the present so that you can have a better future.

Be wise with your credit and keep it in

good standing. It's a good rule of thumb to use credit for small expenses to build it up, and only for emergencies thereafter. Once you have a good score you can leverage it to obtain assets. The good thing about credit is when you pay your balance off you get the same spending power back of the dollar amount you just paid off.

If you are to buy something or a material thing with credit it's a good idea to make sure its something that will make you money or something that will pay for itself over time as an investment. Learn as much about money as possible and always look for sources that teach you about saving techniques, what options you have to grow your money, and wise investments for the future.

Control Your Own Dollar-

It can be detrimental for Black people to only have one source of income. Nothing's wrong with being career oriented as not every Black person is built to be a full-time business owner. Although entrepreneurship may not be for you, it can be harmful for one in the long term if they are only have one source of income.

Having multiple streams of income or diversifying your income will not only put more money in your pocket, but you will become more flexible in the options you have because you aren't just relying on one income to hold you over. One income can be for taking care of important things, and another income can be used to save up or buy the things you want.

It doesn't matter if its a side hustle that you came up with or if you are investing into someone else's business, a Black person is more power when they have more income opportunities. Many Black professionals deal with a lot of stigma in their career paths and another form of income can be a way of escape in case you may have to make a decision between your integrity and happiness or your money. With the right side hustle or investment you can walk away from a job in which you do not feel respected.

Some Black people have good careers in which they enjoy and have fulfillment, however in this case its still smart to have a side hustle or another form of income in place. Although we can control where we work, rarely can we control the job itself. A Black person may be promoted based on hard work yes, but its usually the decision of someone else if you get a raise or promotion.

You could love you job but if your industry changes, the organizations you work for gets restructured, and or you end up with a new supervisor, you could very well lose your job. Or perhaps you may not like the work environment after whatever change may happen. When you have a job many factors come into play whether you will retain that job. When you work a job always have an exit strategy so you don't fell like you are stuck working where you don't want to. Black people must have a form of income they can control on their own just in case things don't work out on the job.

The book "Rich Dad Poor Dad" by Robert Kiyosaki is a good read for every person. It gives details about the 4 different ways to make money (employee, self employed, business, and investor) and ways in which you can transition from employed/ self employed to the business/ investor end. Kiyosaki breaks down the difference between a liability (which takes money from you) and asset (which brings money to you).

Theirs many Black people who are very fiscally responsible, however theirs still a large population of Black people who buy liabilities as if they were assets. If you don't want to go through the stress of running a business, you can invest money into a business in exchange for equity or ownership in the business. You can do this as an investor. Even if your investments give you a small percentage on your return, the gains can add up over time if you let it build. You can invest in several companies you believe in and have other people do the hard work for you.

This means you can invest in companies that are on the rise. If you would prefer to take less of a risk then, you can invest in the stock market and buy shares of trusted already established businesses. You do however stand to make more money from new businesses on the rise, however this is more risky than investing in big name companies. Not only can companies grow money for you depending on their performance in the market, they can also provide income for you in the form of dividends, which is a set amount that the businesses pay to their shareholders for as long as they possess the stock.

Whether its stocks, a business you start, or

even just a side hustle, you need to find another form of income that someone else is not in control of. If Black people are enslaved to money and occupation, than we have not achieved progress, we have just traded in an old master for a new one.

Saving Money-

To properly save you must know what you are saving for so you will be inspired to be disciplined enough to put the money aside. One should save for long term goals like retirement, future emergencies, and for your offspring or the youth in your family. One should also save for short-term goals like investments, paying off debts, and saving for the things you want.

Saving money allows you to gain more leverage over your life. If you save long enough and are disciplined enough not to touch your savings and let it grow you can stop yourself from living from check to check. It will also allow you to be more comfortable and prepared when emergencies or sudden expenses pop up.

If all your income for living comes from the payment of a job you will have less leverage in governing your own life if you do not save. Saving through a 401k or Social Security is fine, however stipulations and regulations with these vehicles can change in ways that are out of your control. The goal of every Black person is to get to a point where you can control your own dollars.

"You only live once, I should be able to buy SOMETHING for myself!"

Saving for Wants-

Another good aspect of saving that doesn't get mentioned often enough, is that the more you save for the future, the more flexibility you can be with the money you presently have. If you have a comfortable amount saved up, you will be able to better recover and spend in comfort on things you want. When you have good savings backing you, it will allow you to spend on the things you want without hurting your finances.

If you haven't saved for long and don't feel like you have saved enough to buy on impulse, then it may be a good idea to have a savings account or holding for the things you want. Instead of the risk of putting yourself in financial ruin over wants, save for them. Putting small increments or a desired amount in "want savings" will allow you to save and buy the things you want but maybe don't need.

Your financial life comes down to sorting expenses into groups of wants and priorities. Priorities should always come first and where most of your spending power should go. Saving for wants can allow us to enjoy our money without feeling guilty about it. Once again treat your want's and desires like a bill. Once you've reached your goal or desired amount, you can spend money on wants without sacrificing the money you need to take care of your priorities.

Multiple Forms of Saving

Multiple forms of income allows us to

make money from multiple sources, saving money should be thought of the same way. Not only should you allocate saving for multiple purposes, but you should also have multiple ways of saving. Saving in one form alone can be dangerous if that form of savings becomes unavailable.

For example if your savings is just in one savings account, and for whatever reason if you cannot access your accounts or your accounts gets frozen, you will be cut off from your savings.

One should save in as many forms as possible. One should save with bank accounts like savings accounts, trust, and CD's. One should also save at home outside of a bank because you never know what could happen to a bank and how if could affect your accounts. Save at least 10% of your earnings at home in a jar or safe a place every time you get paid. It's also a good idea to save change as you are less temped to touch your savings when in the form of loose change, which can surprisingly add up over time. Saving coins in a juice bottle alone can add up to $100 to almost $300 of spending power depending on the size of the container you are using. Even if you prefer to save at home, you should still diversify your savings in case something happens to your home.

In 2023 theirs plenty of apps that allows us to save automatically and manually. The balance to which you have saved up to is always visible on your phone and you can manually add funds to whichever accounts at any time. Another genius things about these apps is that you can label what you are saving for like: "funds for a new house" for example.

If you make income in multiple forms, you will be even more empowered if you save in multiple ways as well. Saving can be easier said than done, but it is an investment for your future self and others to live a more comfortable life.

Multiple Forms of Income:

Just as the popular saying goes "don't put all your eggs in one basket." Reason being, if you drop the basket, you will break all your eggs in that one basket! Its the same with money. You should never have all your income come from one place. Just as we spoke of saving in multiple ways, you should be getting money in multiple ways. Theirs no such thing as job security. Any job or situation can change at any moments notice.

In mid 2019 many people thought they would be okay as long as they had a nice job. The COVID 19 Pandemic has showed us all that work and jobs are never a guaranteed thing. Theirs many who thought they had guaranteed income because they were employed. With the pandemic in full swing, many were frantically looking for help, many of which from government assistance because their job was either shut down or taken away all together.

The pandemic should be a lesson that even a job you love that has the perfect conditions and work atmosphere can be taken away from you by elements that are out of your control. No matter if you are employed or own a business, you should always have more than 1 form of income.

Multiple forms of income allow you to be flexible, recover from losses, and it better positions you to gain more forms of income if you choose. Every person should work to at least have 3 forms of income. If you maintain a traditional job while having multiple forms of income, it can take pressure off of just relying on one. If you do not like the job you are working at, a form of income can help you move on from that job without risking financial turmoil.

Some in the corporate world are able and willing to capitulate into the corporate environment with no problem. However a Black person may not be willing to compromise self or culture in no aspects. Black people should not have to act outside of themselves or their culture to maintain a living.

Our ancestors had to put up with and accept such ideologies to help provide for their families. Black people in 2024 owe it to your ancestors who had to endure a lot of scrutiny on the job just to maintain a career not to endure the same pain or treatment. If we do so we are not advancing forward.

Having another form of income is a good way to make sure you never have to be trapped into putting money and livelihood over pride and respect. To do such a thing is commendable to an extent, however how long one is willing to deal with such treatment varies from person to person. If a Black person feels disrespected on the job or feels undervalued, you have duty to strive for better. Black people owe it to their ancestors to demand better treatment and to not put up with what generations before had to deal with. Having another form of income will empower you to walk away from any corporate job that does not respect you.

Pay Your Bills In Increments

The normal way that most people pay bills is they get an invoice in the mail or email and they pay the requested amount in due time. Doing this for one bill sounds like a doable thing but it can be stressful to account for all your bills at once in this manner. Instead of paying bills by lump sums, put small payments on your bill every time you get paid or a set amount each specific day of the week of your choosing.

Trying to pay multiple bills in full at once cannot only be stressful but leave one financially strapped considering one's situation. Even weekly installments can add up and have you pay noticeably less than what you would instead of waiting until the balance is due.

In today's world (2023 and beyond) most bills can be paid electronically, meaning you can make payments on these bills at any time. As soon as you get paid and save for long term/short term goals, you should then put some payment on one of your bills. You are better off lessening the burden making payments throughout the month, instead of trying to take care of all your bills in full all at once.

Educate Yourself On Money

An ambitious person knows theirs always more to learn about everything, this includes money. Study books, articles, and videos that show you beneficial ways to make, invest, save, and protect your money.

Know and understand the importance of credit and make arrangements to pay off any past debt. Think of credit as your friend and not something to be afraid of. Understand that when you pay off a credit bill the same amount of money is available for spending once again. If you can pay it back, you can spend it again. If you withdraw money from your bank to pay bills whatever you paid is gone until you can replace what you spent. Understand what will lower and increase your credit score and how credit can be used to your advantage.

Creating a business LLC (Limited Liability Company) can separate your personal name and responsibility from your business which can be very beneficial and even position you to have a separate line of credit. Incorporating your business can provide even more protection against your personal name and assets.

When you form a business LLC or corporation, banks will offer you business banking accounts and credit cards. You will also get opportunities and deals on items from companies you may have never heard of. As of 2021, one can get loan offers from *Pay Pal* and *Square* business accounts just by having a consistent flow of sales and income. Some of these opportunities do NOT require credit approval.

When saving money for offspring or anyone in the family, the money that is saved can be put into a trust which will only be accessible to a stated beneficiary of the trust only. This means that money in a trust cannot be taxed, or accessed by creditors if formed the right way. When you know how to raise, save, and protect your money you will feel more comfortable investing your money and using your money to make money for you.

Life insurance can also be helpful in giving money to loved ones after you pass away. Until that point it can be something you can borrow a loan against over time depending on your policy.

Knowing where to invest your money can lead to major payouts for you in the future. Investing in the right stocks, buying equity in the right businesses, and placing your money in the right industries at the right times can very beneficial. The knowledge of these investments can be found by staying up to date on finances and actively educating yourself on the issue. Theirs no guarantee for any investment you make but as long as you can gain, save, and protect your money you will be able to recover from the risk of investing.

Buy Black

The dollars we give in exchange for goods reap benefits for the recipients of those funds. For that reason, its important that Black people use their money at Black establishments. The person you spend with is the person who will benefit from your money. Using your money at Black establishments is way to help Black people without being on the front line of activism.

If you want to see your people do well, make sure you are participating in the community and not just a part of it. It is a good practice for Black people to put Black businesses as the priority of spending then the best possible choice then after.

How Does Fiscal Responsibility Break Barriers?:

When Black people earn more money, save more money, and become more intentional on where they spend their money and what they spend it on, it benefits the entire community when done on a mass level. When Black people become more intentional with their money, they will do more things that will benefit their community.

Also, when you know how to be fiscally responsible you can teach it to others. Imagine how the Black community could move if more become financially intelligent. When this type of knowledge can be passed on to others it can benefit them for rest of their lives. When we can learn from each other and support each other, the walls that separates will come tumbling down.

- Constantly study ways to make, save, and invest money.

- Get organized with your money and save for priorities, emergencies, investment opportunities, and for leisure.

- Save and spend with a purpose.

- Have more than one way to save money.

- Have more than one form of income.

- If you have a career/job, have income outside of your work.

- Teach financial literacy to your children, the young people in your family, the youth around you, and your peers.

- Spend your money at Black owned establishments first, and as often as possible.

WE WILL
SUPPORT BLACK
BUSINESSES

Supporting Black businesses is one of the most important things you can do. When you support a Black business, you are putting money where a Black person can benefit in some way shape or form.

A family can support themselves off of your money. Its important to keep a Black business running because more than likely they will hire Black employees meaning supporting such businesses ensures more jobs for Black people.

Supporting Black business also gives greater possibilities of brands and businesses that are beneficial to the community. In some markets and fields people of color go unrepresented. If we want products geared towards Black people with ethical marketing its best if it comes from a Black creator.

One big issue that Black people face is the reality of having to find work mostly from people of other ethnic backgrounds who have dominated an industry. If the community wants to see representatives of their race control an industry or be at the top of an industry, they will need a lot of support.

In this world representation means a lot. One can believe in possibilities with no examples, but its even easier to see yourself accomplishing something when someone who looks like you is successful. There's nothing like seeing an example of what you want or want to be in the flesh. Black people need to see Black businesses operate and be successful so that others will be inspired to do the same. Most stereotypes concerning Black people are negative and the stereotypes of Black people doing business is no better. They are stereotyped as being unprofessional, unstable, and not long lasting. Community support will put all those stereotypes to rest.

"But black owned businesses are so unprofessional!"

Are some Black owned businesses unprofessional? Yes, of course, so are some Latino, Asian, and White owned business. The difference is that the stigma of Black businesses is so strong that many Black people buy into these negative stereotypes. This causes Black people to be "one and done", which means a Black business get's one chance to get it right, where sadly businesses owned by other races get multiple chances to get it right.

Any and every issue that one could have with a Black owned business, the same could be experienced with a business from someone else of another ethnic background. The reason why the community should give Black businesses multiple chances because theirs fewer Black business owners in most industries outside of our interest. In order to have a strong community the people must have businesses and representation in as many areas of human life; art, technology, education, agriculture, energy, science, sports, development industries and more.

A sad story was written in the passage of Carter G. Woodson's book *"The Mis-Education of the Negro"*. The author of the book recounted a story where a White owned store in a predominately Black neighborhood was approached by Black leaders in the community. They demanded that the store owner put a Black person in charge as a manager at the store. The White man honestly told him that it would do no good because Black people would prefer **NOT** to deal with a Black manager.

The community leaders still insisted that he hire a Black manager, and despite the Caucasian store owners concerns, he hired a Black manage to sadly be proven right. They found out that a good number of Black people in the neighborhood objected to dealing with a manager who looked like them. The people in the neighborhood did not trust a Black man/ woman's business practices and preferred White businesses and White managers despite discrimination and racism.

To be fair this is just one example, in one neighborhood, in the 1930's- 1940's. However many people in 2023 think with this mindset. I cannot say that all Black people think this way, however too many think of Black business or Black success in this fashion; "if its white its right."

Black businesses will not get better if you just simply give up on them. If you have unpleasant experiences with Black owned businesses go and talk to a supervisor so they can address the issue. If you can't talk to a supervisor, send an email. Some issues can be resolved with minor adjustments, if given a chance.

The "White is Right" Conditioning-

Many from the Black community are

quicker to support non-Black business because for many it is seen to be more official, top of the line, and/or thought of to be a better choice. Some Black people are convinced that business or ideas that come from White people are more valuable. These ideas sway Black people into constantly shopping with business owners of other races while shopping with Black owned businesses with skepticism.

Every race on the planet has offered great contributions to mankind, and Black people are no different. If you study Black history in America you will find Black people were behind some of the most brilliant inventions, innovations, businesses, brands, and revolutionary ideas. Studying Black history in business and gaining a strong sense of self will help a Black person support their peers in business.

"Cool, I need you to hook me up"

Looking for the "hook up" or deals every time you shop Black is detrimental to the community and the culture. You should want to pay full price so that the business is fully supported. To ask a Black business for a discount that you wouldn't ask of a business owned by another race of person is pathetic. When supporting a business keep in mind that not only are you buying a product or services but you are supporting the people behind the business as well. How can a Black business stay open if everyone is getting discounts? Black people have a lot of spending power, to be a cheap-skate with your own people's business is an abomination.

Actively Seek Black Business

Hungry? Well next time you go out to eat look up a Black own restaurant. Any of your business needs look for a Black owned business that offers the same or similar product/ service. When you go on vacation always look for Black owned alternatives first before shopping anywhere else. This isn't about being racist to other business owners, its about supporting your community first, no malice intended. Of course theirs nothing wrong with spending with people of other races, just always keep in mind who needs your support the most.

- Eat at Black owned restaurants.

- Actively seek Black owned businesses to spend at first for all your needs.

- Support those you know who have opened a business.

- Promote and spread the word of good service you've experienced at Black owned places.

- If you have a bad experience at a Black owned businesses contact management and express your concerns. Do **NOT** condemn all other Black businesses because you had negative experiences with one or a few Black owned businesses.

- When you travel, actively seek Black owned businesses to patronize.

- If you have an idea and the drive, start a business especially if it benefits others.

WE WILL CREATE OUR OWN BUSINESSES

Like stated in the law before, there's too many benefits afforded to Black people when they become entrepreneurs. Having some form of self-income whether its full time, part time, and or residual basis is empowering. Running a business allows you to create your own income, control your own income, provide effort to any cause you wish. You have the option to do something you like and/or have interest in.

Starting and maintaining a business may be one of the toughest things you've ever done, but if you stay on your path, provide value, and build a strong team, you will gain some of the time back that it took you to build the business. The goal of every business owner should be to get your business to a self-sustaining point where you can take yourself out of the business. Once your business is at a self- sustaining point, you are more free to maneuver as you wish and work towards other things in your interest. Most jobs will have employees on a fixed income meaning you will be getting the same pay every pay cycle until you get a raise. Most people I know say they barely notice a pay increase when getting a raise. A job or career is a stable form of income yes, however Black people must be free to pursue whatever dollar amount in theirs desire, not just what employment offers.

Black people must always keep in mind what accomplished author Claude Anderson said in a video interview with activist Boyce Watkins:

"Rights and Privileges come from what you own and control."

A good majority of Black people are earning their income from corporations owned by others outside of the community. Some of these companies are good places to work. However some Black people find that their work identity may clash with their cultural identity. **Cora Daniels** said it best in her book *Black Power Inc.*:

"Earning respect in the office, as a Black executive, is more of a battle than expected. Also the daily struggle of trying to fit into corporate environments that reward conformity can be trying for any group that is different."

Some can fit into the corporate world no problem, while others force themselves to fit in although they may not want to. Then theirs others who cannot fit into the confines of the corporate world. Theirs no right or wrong here, it all depends on the type of person you are. We now live in a time where its easier than ever to be a business owner, so Black people do not have to live up to the standards of corporations.

Find Your Reason Why:

Your reason for going into business is one of the most important steps to take. Your reason will motivate you to start, maintain, and reach your goals you set forth. Not only will it motivate you to start, but it will also keep you in the game when things get tough. Business will not be easy all the time, so your reason *why* is going to be what keeps you in business.

Make sure your reason is bigger than material means. Material means can be part of your motivation, but it should not be your only motivation. If you make your son or daughter your motivation for going into business, you will be a lot more motivated to succeed than if you are just in it for items.

When you want to start something that benefits others you will start to think with the mindset; *this **HAS** to work*! Nothing is wrong with creating an asset to pay for a liability, however if you are just starting out you should use the most powerful form of motivation you can think of. For most people these are things far beyond material possessions. In my opinion, you will go further when your work benefits other people and the communities of your choosing.

Full Time Business Owner

This type of business owner is vital to the growth and development of the Black community. This is putting all your efforts, knowledge, and resources at work to create your own business and form of income. Their will be risk involved but if you think with the mindset that taking losses is a part of the journey to prepare you for the better, you will be able to see successful days. Always remember if you are afraid to fail you are also afraid to succeed.

The lessons you will learn along the way will help you in the future if not be useful advice to someone else or the youth. You can hand down and share your business intellect to members of your family or whoever you choose. If you should be talented, diligent, and persistent enough you may be able to empower your family with your business or even pass it down to your offspring when you feel the time is right.

You will be working towards something of your desire or interest making all the risk worthwhile. You may even want to invest in a business that you may not be interested in, but it is profitable. Always remember you do not have to be apart of a business to start a business. For example, you do not have to be a barber or know how to cut hair at all in order to own a barber shop. Most businesses are going to be tough in the beginning, but you may be amazed by the support you may gain from members in your community. You will be empowered to get behind any cause you so choose, not the one a job demands.

Part Time/ Side Hustle-

One does not have to be a full-time business owner; you can work a business on the side of maintaining a full time job. Maybe you are not ready to be a full-time business owner or maybe you do not have the desire to be a full time business owner. Nothing's wrong with being a career-oriented person but for the sake of leverage of self, it's always a good idea for every Black career person to have some sort of income outside of their job.

Black people can sometimes deal with racism and oppression on the job, having a hustle on the side allows for one to be in a better position to walk away from a job if they want to. Any passive income that allows you to make money outside of the specific job will due. One of the worst situations a person can be in is having to accept racial overtones because they have no other source of income.

Having a part time job also allows you to make more money which can lighten the burden of bills. You can also use the income to spend on wants while your job income fulfills your needs. Money from your part-time job can grow your business so it can become your full-time job. Having more income will allow you to gain more leverage making it possible for you to have more control of your life. Be warned that getting a second job that trades time for money will take more of your time and energy away from doing the things that you want to do.

If you have more than one job, I think its best that the second job is temporary and being used to make a certain amount of money or to obtain a certain goal. Most people I know who have more than one job, can only do such a thing for so long before they get burnt out. Always remember, your mental and physical health will always be more important than any work you do. If you are to work more than one job as an employee, always have an exit strategy. Do not feel like you are doing a company a dis-service doing this. Companies are using you for their interest, so do not feel guilty when using them to get what you need or want. Making a semi-passive form of income, is usually a better idea than to get a second job.

Investor-

Being an investor is a unique position to be in because instead of you doing work in a business it allows for your money to work for you. In this type of business model, you invest in people and/or a system which not only does the work of business for you, but allows you to make money while doing other things you may want or need to do. Every entrepreneur and career-oriented person should aspire to reach the investor level of business.

Invest In Your Ideas-

Investing money into your ideas and plans is a critical element in bringing your business to life but it is not the only ingredient to make your business profitable. You also must be willing to invest time, energy, creativity, and faith into your endeavor. In order to keep growing in business you must constantly grow in your field of business and as an individual. One should be constantly reading books, studying, taking on mentors, and knowing as much as possible about the business they're in.

Living in a world that is oppressive towards them, Black people should always want to know the perspective of business from a Black person. I look for great advice for being a business owner wherever it is available. The book *The Power of the Subconscious Mind* by **Joseph Murphy** isn't focused around business alone but theirs quite a few beneficial passages on the topic. For people starting out in business the book has 3 steps that people should consider before starting a business. 1, Find your purpose in business, 2 specialize in a specific area, and 3 make sure your business benefits others.

Make Sure Others Can Benefit From Your Business:

All of the 3 steps mentioned in *The Power of the Subconscious Mind* are very important, but for Black people emphasis has to be put on the third step of make sure your business benefits others. While we try to become more united and powerful as a community our business endeavors must be beneficial. This means the product or service provided to customers should benefit them, your business should also provide opportunities for others to gain income or gain experience in a field that will benefit their future.

Do not be overly selfish in your pursuit of business. Too many Black people are trying to outdo the next Black person to compare accomplishments or success. A Black person should never pursuit success in business in the hopes of rubbing it in the face of another Black person.

You should work to make opportunities available to others and use your success to uplift the community, not to look down at another because they don't have as much as you do. Someone who lacks self-love and self-esteem may always feel necessary to compare himself/herself to the next person. Usually, the Black person who has high self-love and self-esteem would prefer to be a provider to Black people not an antagonist.

- Assess where you currently work as ask yourself ; *"Am I happy here? Am I respected here by supervisors and peers"*, and lastly *"Is this work fulfilling to me?"*

- Figure out if you are happy and want to stay on your job, or if you would like to do something else. If you have interest in other endeavors, develop an exit strategy.

- Have a valid reason why you will go into business. This will be your foundation, you motivation to keep going, and the reason why you won't quit.

- If you have a career or job develop another form of income independent of where you currently work, preferably a side hustle or a business instead of getting a second job.

- If you do decide to start a business determine what level of involvement you would like to take part in the business. Do you want to be full-time, part-time, or do you want to be an investor?

- If you proceed with opening a business, become a student of the craft you are in and gain as much knowledge as possible about the craft and good general business practices.

- If possible make sure your business either is something you are passionate about, good at doing, or have knowledge of. You may pursue a business that you are not passionate about, however make sure that it fuels something you have passion for. This will allow you to stay motivated when things get tough.

- Make sure your business can and will benefit others in your community.

WE WILL NETWORK WITH EACH OTHER

The goal in mind is to build with each other, not to compete against each other. Any business idea you have in mind can go further with the help of others. The best situations as far as business and networking among Black folks is a situation where both parties benefit equally. A win -win opportunity should be paramount when Black people seek to do business with each other.

Ways Of Networking:

Give Support-

If you want support, you have to give support. On social media you can easily share a friend or family member's business or ideas to help them gain clientele. Even for businesses who have owners that's you don't know personally, if you experienced good service show your gratitude and share the business on social media and refer to friends. Considering where Black people stand in America and in many places around the world, EVERY Black person should be promoting another Black person's business!

If you aren't social media savvy, simply sending a few text message pictures to a few people you know who would be interested in the service is an effective means of networking and at the very least showing support. Doing these simple tasks cost you nothing and takes little time. Another means of networking is doing business with each other.

Buy products from small businesses and make it an active effort to support them just as much as the big conglomerates we all support daily. Once again if you want others to buy from you, you have to buy from others. If you are in business, you may want to partner with other businesses to gain more income together.

Partnership-

A partnership is as simple as joining forces to get money together. This can be done as a business partnership, or you can collaborate with another company to throw a bigger, more successful event than what you could do by yourself. If you are doing business on agreeable terms, and both parties are bringing equivalent work or resources into the partnership good things can happen. Both of you can decide if the partnership will be a one time venture, on occasions, or for a extended period of time.

A key element to partnerships is communication. Both sides must know and understand the details of responsibilities, how money will be spent, and specific factors depending on what type of business you are doing. Look at each other as equals and operate as so. A partnership among Black people simply just must be a win-win situation.

My Experience:

Since being in Atlanta I've had to partner up with many other Black business owners in the city. Not all partnerships have panned out well but more often than not, most of the partnership experiences with other Black business owners have been extremely positive and productive. I've been able to grow in business with long term business partners and partners I'm on an event-by-event basis with.

Any setbacks I've personally dealt with were minor instances that could have been experienced with dealing with anyone of any other race. When doing business with someone long enough sometimes things will go wrong or not according to plan. This is normal in general when it comes to business regardless of race.

Not only have I had supportive partners in my businesses, but the majority of my customers are Black and support my business as well. I've gotten good referrals and have been sought out to do corporate events by Black professionals. Many of my partners have come from both direct communications, but mostly through finding each other on social media. My experience as a Black business owner showed me that Black business does work, we do support each other, we can work well together, and we do have a future.

- Actively support Black owned businesses. Make it a point to support business owners you know and those you don't know.

- Share and promote small businesses among friends and social media.

- For business owners, network with each other to do events on a larger scale.

- Network to build events and services that benefit the surrounding communities in your area.

WE WILL PROTECT OURSELVES

I love Anime! I watched a amazing anime movie series, called **Berserk**, one of the main characters saved a woman from being raped. He then said something that has stuck with me: "If you have something to protect, take up the sword." Given the history and present that Black people have to deal with, the people must be willing to individually protect themselves and their families.

Black people should aspire to arm themselves mentally and physically. History has shown for the most part, that whenever Black people culturally reach a point of satisfaction, (as much as I hate to say it) we tend to become complacent in the areas of warfare and self-defense.

Mental Protection-

Being mentally protected is simply knowing the knowledge that will protect you from harm from others. This means knowing your history, the contributions made by your people, the historic oppression/ harm that has caused issues for your people, knowing the law, how to be in good health, and how you can protect yourself from enemies.

Think to yourself: "How do I feel?" You should have this thought everyday. You may find that you are more tense or stressed out, than you think. Being overly stressed puts a lot of strain on your body. Stress causes your body to go into fight of flight mode. This is a primal reaction to stress preparing the body to either fight or run away from danger. Just like how one could tear and harm muscles when they are overworked, the human body is the same way. Put too much strain on your mental capacity and it will cause harm to your health mentally and physically.

Taking care of your mental health mean relieving yourself of stress in a healthy way. You have to relieve this stress without turning to something that can harm you like drug addiction. Whether its meditation, exercise, art, or an activity you like, find something that help you relieve stress. Rest and relaxation will allow your body to repair and perform when you needed.

Self Esteem:

How do you feel about yourself? Is your self talk positive or negative? How you feel about yourself plays a major role in the actions you take in life and your overall health in general. Make sure you are giving yourself positive self-talk, even if you have to talk to yourself aloud. Words are powerful, whether you speak or write them. You may be surprised how the words you speak and write can come to pass.

Make sure you have a positive image of yourself in your head. Speak words of motivation to yourself. Having good self-esteem, good self-talk, and a positive image of yourself, will allow you to stay in a good place mentally when others try to attack you with their words and thoughts. Just as you must defend yourself against physical attacks, you must be able to defend yourself from being attack by others from a mental standpoint.

You cannot allow for others, the media, and even family and friends, to destroy good self esteem you have for yourself. No matter what you face in life, your mental health is always in your control, and you will forever have the power to alter it how you see fit. If you are in complete control over your mental health, always make sure it works towards your benefit.

Like anything else, you can become better at something the more you study the subject. Learning is one of the best ways to protect yourself. Learn new defense techniques, new ways to relieve stress, and learn from your history.

History:

As the great saying goes "If you do not know your history, you are doomed to repeat it." The job of every Black person, no matter what their occupation may be, is to make sure their peers and generations after never have to face the same oppression previous generations had to deal with. One of the best ways to position the community in a better place is to understand how the people are being oppressed from a historic and current standpoint.

The mistakes of the people before us give us a blueprint of what to avoid in the future. The best thing about knowing your history is that you can give brief summaries of important events and perspectives to people who may be ignorant to the knowledge you can provide. Just by knowing history you can help others in their growth process.

Physical Ability-

If you had to fight for your life right now, would you be able to? If you had to run for your life or run to get help, would you be able to? These are the questions that human beings living on earth should ask. Every person should be physically fit enough to defend themselves if need be. This does not mean you have to be a body builder or a personal trainer.

This means being in good enough shape to be able to defend yourself and the people you love. Before you can physically defend yourself, you must be in good physical shape. Be warned, although arming yourself with gun is encouraged, you cannot protect yourself with a gun all the time. Once again, the ways in which you are fit, you can break barriers by helping and inspiring others to reach their fitness goals.

Physical Defense:

Fighting Defense-

Given the historic and present-day systematic oppression facing Black people collectively, Black people do not have the luxury to not know ways of defending family and self. Learning how to defend yourself or how to fight is not about attacking someone but should be used for self-defense purposes only.

This means that every Black person should learn some form of boxing, martial arts, and how to use a firearm. The legendary Bruce Lee said there's no style of martial arts that is the best. It's important to choose the style that works best for you. Whether its karate, muay Thai, Boxing, or Mixed Martial Arts is your choice. Lee also said it's better to find the style that's best for you. What matters most is that you have the means to protect yourself above all.

From a historic standpoint many Black Americans were abused mentally and physically since being forced into slavery in the United States, through the Jim Crow and the Civil Rights Era. There's nothing weak about our ancestors. In many times of physical altercations based on race, Black people were not only outnumbered, but it was once a law that a Black person can be imprisoned for hitting a White person for any reason.

We must always be proud of the horrors our ancestors had to endure so that we can live in better circumstances today. We must be sure that our people collectively never have to experience the horrors our ancestors experienced. Every Black person needs to find a gym or dojo where they can learn self-defense techniques and practice sparring. One can even create a gym at home if you do not want to travel. Study self-defense and take it seriously because your life may depend on it.

Teaching Self Defense to Children

Teaching self-defense techniques to children is just as important as them learning math, science, and financial literacy. If a parent is experienced in self-defense techniques themselves, it is encouraged that they teach

194

valuable techniques to their children. If you are not experienced in self-defense as a parent, then you and your children should take martial arts or boxing classes.

Black children will face the same stigma in this world that Black adults will face. Black children should be informed on how to defend themselves against adults. Some from the community can become too comfortable, thinking that they will not face dangers because they may be rich or successful. Some think they are 100% safe because they live in a good neighborhood. NEVER think this way. There is no such thing as absolute safety anywhere for anyone. This is especially true for Black people who have to face stigma around the globe. As a community we must be able and willing to fight for our freedoms and rights at all times. Like stated earlier violence is not being encouraged, but Black people in this world must be prepared, no exceptions.

Arm Yourself

Every Black person should own a gun of some type, no exceptions. Preferably a Black person should own a firearm that should be kept at the house and a gun you should be able to have in your car when you are mobile (if your state allows for it legally). Not only is it important to own a gun but you must have knowledge of how to shoot a gun properly and how to clean and manage a gun. Just like fighting styles in self-defense, theirs no perfect gun to have. You should aim to own a firearm you are comfortable with. If you are unfamiliar with different types of guns, you can go to your local shooting range and rent a variety of guns to see which works best for you.

Its a good idea to own a big gun for the house like a shotgun or riffle, while you should own a pistol for your car or when you are on the go. Never forget that Black ancestors were once dragged out of their own homes and lynched by members of the Ku Klux Klan and the police did nothing about it. We all must stay armed to protect ourselves.

Just as Black children should be introduced to self-defense by parents, they should also be taught how to shoot a gun and proper gun management. Of course, it should be stressed that a gun should never be used unless in an extreme defensive situation. Parents should give children scenarios of when it is a proper time to use a gun.

If a parent is lacking knowledge in such a field, then one can always seek out firearms training from professionals. This of course is up to the desertion of parents when the proper age is to introduce your offspring to such a thing, but self-defense should be taught to all Black offspring, no exceptions.

Other Forms of Protecting Ourselves:

Black people protecting themselves goes way beyond physical threat or attack. What would you do if every bank shut down right now? What would you do if every grocery store ran out of food? Would you be able to survive a catastrophic event right now?

Financial Protection-

Protecting one's money is just as important as protecting one's physical being, because money helps one keep their physical being in good standing. It's smart to have money in the bank, but not all of your money in the bank. It's a good idea to have multiple places to store money both digitally and physically. Of course, money in the bank allows you to make purchases by card and online however if you ever have issues with one financial institution, you will not want all your money to be there.

Have multiple places to put your money means, multiple bank accounts with different banks, and keeping savings digital funds in apps like *Cash App* and *PayPal.* It is also ideal to keep cash on yourself and kept somewhere at home in a safe place. Cash should be put in the most secure discrete location (preferably only known to you). Investing in a safe may be a good idea. Saving cash somewhere else along with a safe is also a good idea so that all your cash is not in an obvious place.

Having money available to your disposal in multiple locations will allow you to recover and bounce back just in case you have issues with one of the places you have money. Having accounts separate for bills, business, and personal use is all a smart way to organize your money.

A portion of your money should be saved for emergencies, another portion should be used to invest in a vehicle that can make you more money whether its a business, a tool/

instrument, or stocks.

Putting your money in *trust* allows for money to be saved for a designated family member that will inherit the money when you pass away. Another good vehicle to place your money for saving is a custodial Roth IRA accounts. Some of these accounts are best for self-employed retirement, while others are geared for inheritance. Both of which allow for a safe form of long-term saving. You must do your due diligence to see how taxes and creditors could affect these accounts. Stocks may go up and down with the market, but also usually see a good return on investment over an extended period of time.

It's good to have a diverse stock portfolio of big-name stock or blue-chip stocks (Google, Amazon, Tesla) and stocks from up and coming companies. You can invest long term in stocks of big-name companies that are least likely to crash, and you can invest stocks into business that are on the way up for short term gain that you can sale when you please. It's a good idea to invest in stocks to keep long term and stocks you want to sale in order to make money.

Stocking Key Items-

Protecting yourself means being prepared to face the worst-case scenario and survive it. This means stocking water and food you can keep as reserve items just in case grocery stores can't provide you with food. Foods like lentils, quinoa, beans, rice, oatmeal, peanuts, spring water granola bars, peanut butter, and canned food items. Canned food items would be the least desired because of high sodium and preservatives, but in desperate times certain sacrifice may have to be made. Stock items like batteries, flashlights, tool kits, and first aid kits. It is also a good idea to stash seeds of fruits and vegetables you like in a storage area so that you can grow your own food.

Control Your Food

One big key to having a better diet and spending less money on food is cooking and preparing your own food instead of going out to eat. Shopping for food is always better than expecting to eat out all the time, however an even deeper element of control is growing your own food. I prefer not to hunt, but if you must survive on meat, learning effective hunting techniques may be helpful as well.

Putting the production of food in your own hands allows you to better manage your food intake. Allowing our food consumption to come from grocery stores or companies will spell disaster for you if either of which stops serving food. Growing crops should encourage one to eat healthier, which is also a form of defending oneself.

Defend for Destiny

Defending yourself is simply putting your destiny in your own hands. Black people collectively in this lifetime have too many instances in which we are at the control of others. If we want control of our own destiny, we must be defensive minded.

- Know the history of your people so you can know where you need to protect yourself.

- Assess your mental health. Find your mood and stress level. Practice good self-talk and mental visualization of what you would like to accomplish.

- Practice good rest and relaxation techniques. Meditate at least twice a day. Make sure you at least get 6-8 hours of sleep every night.

- Create a workout routine that works for you. If you do not know what workouts to do, you can do research, join a gym, or get a personal trainer.

- Learn self-defense techniques.

- Own a gun and learn how to use it responsibly.

- Stock vital food and items in case of an emergency.

- Save money for emergencies. Save money in bank accounts, on digital apps, on hand, and stashed in a safe discreate location.

- Create your own garden and grow your own food.

- Do NOT become paranoid, but always be mindful of the safety of you and your family.

WE WILL BE HEALTH CONSCIOUS

In order to maintain a strong community its people must be healthy and strong. The key to being healthy is knowledge. Knowing how to be healthy and maintain health, implementation, and discipline. Black people must be equally mindful of both their mental and physical health.

If you do not maintain a balance of good mental and physical health, you run a higher risk of suffering negative consequences. Even if you are in great physical health but have poor mental health you may be faced with negative health consequences. If one spectrum of your health is in poor condition eventually the other will fail as well. Both aspects, mental and physical health, are equally important and should be maintained well to live a better quality of life.

Mental Health:

Mental health is a combination of one's self-esteem, motivation, outlook, and thoughts. If all these factors are in a positive place, one can do wonders. Some Black people grow up in circumstances where they have poor mental health due to the environment they grew up in, and social conditioning if not both. Black people at some point of their lives need to have an honest assessment of their mental health if not done by themselves then professionally. Mental health should be addressed as early as possible in one's life, starting as early as childhood.

Theirs a population of Black people who

are under the assumption they have good personal self-esteem all while having a poor outlook towards people of their own race. Major components of this issue can be solved by understanding Black history outside of a formal educational system.

Self-identification is one of the best ways to build self-esteem. When you know and accept who you are, others will not be able to tear you down or tell you otherwise unless you let them. More of the community needs to know the stories of valor and courage, so they can see themselves as winners and survivors, and not just stories of Black people being victims.

When the community can reject the negative notions that society tries to label Black people with, we are then equipped not to be judgmental of the peers who look like us. Black people need to love themselves even if society or the people around them don't. Confidence comes when the community realizes they do not come from ancestors of inferiority.

They come from a royal, courageous people who made inventions, structures, art, and philosophies that have benefited the world. Even in times of slavery, Reconstruction, the Industrial Revolution, Jim Crow, and the Civil Rights era, there's plenty stories of Black excellence that have taken place in the face of oppression. If these people were able to do wonders while living in a time far more oppressive than present times, why should any Black person doubt themselves in any way?

Knowing the history of your culture beyond what school teaches will help you know yourself and what you come from. Knowing the history of the success of an oppressed people will give you proof that you can do great things. I recommend that every Black person reads *"Think and Grow Rich: A Black Choice"* by **Napoleon Hill** and **Dennis Kimbro**. It gives a good account of Black prominence from slavery to the early 90's that may not be covered in formal education and gives one the keys to having the right mindset and tools for success.

Yet and still, Black history and the history of the people who have originated in Africa and America is broader than what any book can cover, so one must be willing to make learning as much as possible about your people's history. This should be a lifelong endeavor as you can never learn or know enough. Study the history of your people from as many sources as possible; your self-worth will be found.

Your Personal History:

While you continue to learn about the history of your people, make sure you recount your own personal history. What have you been through? What past issues have hindered you or stopped you from achieving what you wanted? In therapy you learn that your past events play a major role in the thoughts and actions you take presently.

Have you ever felt like a victim? If so, change your mind set on the topic. You can choose to be a survivor rather than a victim. Being a survivor allows you to grow from even negative events. Choosing to be a victim will encourage you to hold on to pain, sorrow, and is not as empowering as choosing to be a survivor. Address the areas where you were vulnerable and find healthy ways to protect yourself moving forward. Find what physical and mental needs you must address.

Do not only focus on what you need to improve in, also focus on the times where you were strong and victorious. Think about the times where you came through for others when they were depending on you. Others and the media may try to convey messages to you that may make you doubt yourself.

You have to recall and remember all the times you were triumphant, to remind yourself of how powerful you are. You have to remind yourself "I was strong then!" you have to remember "I made that happen!" This practice is for you to remain confident in yourself and your abilities. How you feel about yourself mentally will play a big factor in how you protect yourself physically.

It's a good idea to seek therapy from a psychiatrist preferably a Black therapist. Of course, there's plenty of therapist of other races who are more than qualified to give you good advice. You'd want a Black therapist for cultural relatability and understanding.

Why You May Still Holding On To "IT":

You may be asking yourself, "why can't I forget about *it*?" We all have that "*it*"; that one bad memory that replays over in our head. We are told we should move on and let go of past negative memories. That sounds great in theory, but what if you just can't let it go.

I shared an epiphany I had with one of my tattoo clients who was going through a tough time. I told her that we hold on to bad memories so we can remember to never feel that way again. When we look back, their probably were ways, we could of prevent ourselves from such pain. We may have seen warning signs that we chose to ignore. Perhaps we could have done things in a better way. Feeling these past moments from time to time can remind us of what we don't want to deal with in the future.

Positive Self-Talk:

The truth is a Black person can go through most their life hearing nothing but negative remarks about them and their people. From the media to your peers, and even your family can speak ill words of you. If you hear nothing but negative talk from people, where can you go to hear positive talk? Go within. Speak positive words of affirmation to yourself.

Your self-talk will influence your mental/ physical health and the words you speak will manifest in the physical world. Negative self-talk will yield negative results, while speaking positive will bring positive results. Always speak highly of yourself and believe in the possibility of achieving great things.

"What if MY voice is the negative voice I hear."

If the negative talk you receive is from your own voice in your head, do not worry. This is not as uncommon as you think, in fact I'm pretty sure such a thing is normal. Whenever you hear your voice making negative statements, counter it with a positive statement. When your voice says, "I can't do this." You can counter with "I can and will do this!" To drown out the negative voice you may have to say it to yourself aloud. Saying positive affirmations to yourself in the mirror is one of the best ways to have a positive outlook.

To be Black means to endure world in a macro telling you that "you are not good enough." This is why positive words and affirmations MUST come from you because theirs no guarantees you will get it from the outside world.

Diet-

Your health is more important than your pursuit of money. Simply fulfilling your hunger pain with any type of food prepared in any type of way and not considering the affects it will have on your health, are eating habits that can lead to illnesses. Unfortunately, Black people have to come to terms that some of the foods we have been traditionally eating for years are no good for our health. Even in most inner-city or urban neighborhoods, most of the eating options will be unhealthy ranging from fast food, processed food stores, and majority fried foods restaurants.

The most important element of diet is knowing what every food you eat does for you and your body. Educate yourselves on what foods give you nutritional values that your body needs to function at a high level. You should eat for benefits, yet many eat on the merits of taste.

Some do what Dr. Africa is calls "emotional eating." This is to eat foods that taste good so you feel good because of the emotional imbalance you are dealing with. Certain foods may trigger memories associated with good times. You may crave these foods when facing hard times which can be an issue when these foods are unhealthy. Instead of eating for nutrition and benefits, most people eat for taste and flavor without thinking about the effects such food will have on their health. It can be tough indeed to deviate from the foods you grew up on, however if it is unhealthy, you should work to remove it from your diet.

A lot of people have the mindset of *"does this taste good?"* instead of *"is this good for me?"* Unfortunately, some of the foods many Black people grew up on and is available around them, is not good for their health. Just like anything else in life, a good diet comes from educating yourself on the subject. It is recommended that you get a book on proper nutrition, however at the very least you can look up healthy foods and their benefits.

Being knowledgeable about food and diet in the Black community is an absolute must because a poor diet has killed more Black people than drugs, gun violence or police brutality. When we were children, our diet depended upon what our parents prepared for us, however as adults we have access to knowledge and the choice of what foods we will eat.

"Man ....I aint trying to give up ribs, chicken wings, and macaroni and cheese. I aint trying to go vegan..."

Although many studies have found that a vegan diet is helpful and many benefits come from such, the goal of this passage isn't to tell you which diet you should be following but to influence to think about what you eat and how it affects you. The goal is to get the community to think in depth about what they are eating, not to tell them what diet they should follow.

By rule of thumb, it is suggested that leafy greens, fruits, and vegetables should be the majority of your diet. Meat and dairy should be least consumed in your diet, in fact many believe one should not consume meat or dairy at all. If you have culinary skills, you can make healthy food taste good. Remember that your body is about 70% water meaning you should drink water more than you eat (preferably spring water). Keep in mind that you can also get your water intake from most fruits and vegetables.

What we drink is also very important to our diet. The majority of your intake should be water, juice should be taken in moderation, while soda (or pop as we call it in the mid-west) and alcoholic drinks should be limited, if even consumed at all. Once again in the same instance many stray away from water in preference of sugary drinks because of taste. Just like eating, one has to think of health benefits when drinking instead of being more concerned with the taste of what you drink. It is said that the human body can live significantly longer on just water than just food alone.

Not all water is the same. Purified water is cleaned with mechanical sources like distilled water however purified water leaves behind minerals while distilled water eliminates contaminates and minerals alike. Lastly spring water is cleaned and comes from a natural source without the use of machines as a filtration system. Spring water is the best choice, because a natural source is best trusted above all.

Eating healthy and staying hydrated not only puts you in good physical health, but it can also improve your mental health as your body and brain will perform better for you. Your health and diet can play a major role on your mental health. When it comes to mental and physical health, one is not more important than the other, both are equally important on the same axis needing to be balanced for good overall health.

Physical Health-

A people who are oppressed should seek strength and power in everything that they do, being in good shape is no different. We must be willing to defend ourselves, family, and others whether we have guns to do it with or not.

Theirs too many benefits in being physically fit for Black people to ignore the issue. When you are fit, you tend to be healthier, most likely you will live longer, and you will be able to do more with your life. You will be able to defend yourself and others. You will tend to be more mentally driven, and you can provide yourself as an example of fitness for the people around you and the youth.

Everyone should be working out at least 3 times a week regardless of age, gender, or circumstances.

"But I'm comfortable with who I am, I have a few extra pounds, but I like it and others like it sooooo......"

Sure, on average people who lose weight tend to be healthier and reduce diseases associated with belly fat, however body acceptance is very important. Nothing's wrong with being heavier than average, the problem is not being physically active. Just because you are a big person does not give an excuse not to work out.

Maybe you don't want to lose weight, which is fine, however it is still imperative for people who have extra weight to work out. Even among big people, those who work out tend to be in better health, they live longer, and still manage to be athletes even if they don't lose any weight. This isn't about body shaming but to inspire all to be physically active regardless of build and body type. A heavy person who works out is putting themselves on a better path than a slim person who never works out.

"Ugh..... I just don't like working out."

If this is the case then do not complain about the detriments that come along with an inactive lifestyle. Don't complain about your health and physical decline that comes along with stagnation. Its best to find a physical activity you enjoy doing so you don't think of being active as "work." You don't have to go to the gym to work out and be active, you can play a game of basketball, soccer, football, swimming, dance, hiking, etc.

Discipline is about doing what's best for you, even when you don't want to or feel like doing it. No matter how great of shape a person is in we all have our days when we don't feel like working out, however those who are able to push past these feelings and manage to stick to their routine anyway seem to be rewarded the best.

"I just don't have the time."

Of course, you have the time to work out, it's just that some people don't WANT to make the time to work out. No matter how tired one is, most people will show up to their jobs no matter what. It doesn't matter how tired they are or if they feel like going, they go because making money is that important to them. Is your health not as important? When it comes to money, we will **find** the will to make money and go to work even when we don't feel like it.

Apply the same mindset to your fitness. It is a job that is just as important as the one you have to make money.

You will have days where you don't feel like working out, but just as you are disciplined enough to pursue money when you don't feel like it, the same discipline needs to be applied to physical fitness. We all have the same 24 hours in a day, yet others manage to still get their workouts in at some point of the day. You say you "don't have time" then make the time. Get up earlier to workout or stay up later to work out. Find a way to get it done or embrace a decline enabling excuse. Whatever money you make will be pointless if your health is not up to par.

If one were to go broke, they can work to get the money they once had and beyond. We all have seen many instances of this. We have also seen people make dramatic improvements in health, that seemed impossible. However, if you ignore your health too long it may be harder to get to a better place if you become ill or sick.

If you lose all of your money you could go broke, if you ignore your health, you could lose your life; which one is worse? Do not embrace excuses that make you ignore your health and physical fitness. It would be a shame for you to make a massive amount of money but then have to turn around and spend it all on medical bills and prescriptions. Everyone living has 2 choices in life; you either will spend time on your health, or spend money on your health, the choice is yours.

Workout Balance

Working out in any way is great! Making the time for it and showing up is something that is commendable because unfortunately a lot do not put forth the effort to do so. However, if you don't have a balanced workout, you can be strong in one area, and that's it.

I notice when I go to public gyms, I see a lot of men work out their upper body and that's it. It screams to me "I'm working out for the look". Nothing's wrong with wanting good looks as a byproduct of working out, however you will get far better results if you also work out for performance.

This means you must exercise your abs, hips, legs, and lower body with the same intensity as your upper body workouts. Some may say you should put more work into building strength in your lower body. I'm and exhibitionist fighter and one thing I can tell you, is one of the worst feelings in a fight, is trying to support yourself and move around on weak legs.

Not only do you want to focus on exercising your entire body, but you also must include walking and/or running. Cardio is important for building up stamina in your muscles, your mental capacity, and building strength in your orans. Imagine having power with no stamina? As a fighter one thing I can tell you is one of the worst feelings in a fight is feeling exhausted and still having to fight, however on the flip side, one of the best feelings in a fight is to notice and realize your opponent is tired but you aren't.

There are also some women who only work out for the looks as well. They can also fall in to traps of limitation as well. Some women who work out for looks alone may become complacent once they've reached a desired point. Some unfortunately, go to the gym for a good picture for social media and won't push themselves any further once getting the right pictures or videos. One will get better results when their goal is to gain a better quality of life from working out as opposed to just working out for looks.

Don't Forget to Stretch

Don't be fooled, there's strength in flexibility! When you are flexible you are less likely to get injured and you have more versatility in the ways you can use your strength and your body. Being flexible keeps the body young and some specific stretches are said to boost testosterone in men.

Range of motion is also important. The movements of muscles, bone, and joints also prevents injury. Range of motion can also build strength in areas that may be hard to address with lifting weights like the hips and groin. Lack of range of motion will cause muscles in the area to become stiff and tight, which could over time lead to you not being able to do certain movements at all. When you start feeling tight, that is when you will feel old. Stretch and move your body as a lifestyle habit and you will benefit in your elder years.

Rest & Relaxation-

Taking time to rest and recover is just as important as being active. In order for anyone's body and mind to work at an optimum level one has to get proper rest. Think of it as the body recovering so you can perform at a high level, with high energy, not just functioning off of what energy you have left over.

Current science suggests you should at least get 6-8 hours of sleep per night. Even taking naps when needed during the day is also suggested. No matter what your craft or job of choice you should take at least one day a week to do as little as possible, rest, and relax. Yes, resting is important for productivity! If you are tired at work, you may miss something important or cut corners all together for the sake of "getting it over with."

There's a difference between working through a tired spell and showing up to the job tired. Your health is your most important asset, make sure you aren't neglecting it or, even worst harming it for some job or someone else.

Make sure you take time to meditate during the day. A good time to meditate is in the morning when you wake up, once during the afternoon and once at night before you sleep. Have envisioning meditations of what you want to accomplish during segments your morning and nighttime meditations. The reason for this is because the subconscious mind is most influenced in the mornings when you first wake and at night before you sleep. Your mediation during the day/afternoon should be a blank thought meditation when you think of nothing but focus on breathing. The day/afternoon meditation is intended to rest your mind.

"How is this supposed to help? All I'm doing is closing my eyes and breathing."

Meditation will rest your mind so you can have more focus and mental energy for the remainder of the day. One may say "Well isn't that what sleep is for?" Yes, sleep is one way to rest, but you may not have the time to get a proper rest. When you meditate you can rest the mind or make impressions on the mind. I'm sure you have had times where you could not focus, forgotten things easily, or felt overwhelmed by your thoughts and/or emotions. Meditation is a helpful solution to all the issues previously mentioned. Author Cyrus Ausar has the perfect metaphor on the benefits of meditation:

"Have you observed a glass of juice that sat for a long time? Did you notice the sugar, the color, and the solid material sank while the top remained clear? If the juice continued to sit long enough, there would eventually be a total separation. Now if that same juice is shaken up, the ingredients will mix back together."

Your mind and thoughts can become clear when you sit in still silence or meditate. If you have too much on your mind or cannot think clearly, it's a good idea to sit in silent stillness and meditate. Since your mind is constantly being stimulated by external and internal forces it's good to include meditation in your daily routine.

Life is best when you can maintain a balance; if you rest, relax, and pamper yourself too much you may become lazy, unmotivated, and unhealthy, however if you are over worked and you do not make time for self-care, you will run your health into the ground. You will find yourself in a good place if you keep a good balance of activity and rest. Both are important and must be equally balanced for you to give your best effort on a day-in-day-out basis.

"Okay this is cool and all, but how is health supposed to "Break Barriers" among black people?"

When you are active, physically fit, health conscious, and live a life of good work/rest balance you become an example for the people around you. When you hold yourself to a standard it can influence others to do the same. You should aspire to be an example to your community, friends, family, and most importantly your children. People do not want to hear your rhetoric on health, they want to see your results.

When you are a good example of health you will become beneficial to people, which will not only break barriers among a group of Black people but can also help them become a team or a group after the same objective.

You don't have to be in perfect shape, but even staying disciplined to a routine can make others ask about what you do and why. This gives you a chance to educate them on better living if they are willing to receive it. Every Black person needs to be able to defend themselves and the community. Being in good shape allows you to do so. Doing good for the people will break the barriers among others who have the same goal. If you are good for the Black community barriers among the people will be broken.

- Create a routine centered around your mental health. To build confidence you must seek knowledge. Know the history of your people and know yourself. What are your triggers?

- Write down your goals. Write down your short term and long-term goals in a place where you can see it every day.

- Create a regiment of meditation (at least once in the morning and once at night), practice positive self-talk, and envision a mental projection of whatever you want to achieve in your mind.

- Meditate at least three times a day. Once in the morning, afternoon, and night.

- Create a workout regiment that is good cardio (running, jogging, and walking) and a routine that builds strength and muscle (weightlifting, calisthenics, and swimming).

- Create a rest and relaxation routine. Make sure you take at least one day off out of the week. Make sure you at least get 6 hours of sleep.

- Be an example of good mental and

physical health for your family, your peers, your community, and most importantly yourself.

WE WILL SEE
EACH OTHER AS
AN ALLY

The" American Way" is to be competitive, compete for a job, a place in business, or a promotion against others, and may the best man/woman win. Black people have to remember that as a race we are collectively and for the most part alone in our climb to prosperity and away from oppression. The "American Way" of doing things may not always work in the favor of Black people, that is when the people have to establish their own way.

Unless you are competing for the same position on a sports team, or for the same role in acting, competition is understandable. When you apply for a job you may even unknowingly compete against Black people who are applying for the same job.

Being competitive in the sense of bringing the best out of each other is great. Competing in a good nature is totally fine. It's the negative thought of competition that we want to stay away from. The type of competition where you hope for the downfall of others.

This type of negative competitive nature may cause one to constantly judge others on everything. Black people collectively and globally do not have the luxury to compete against one another. With the growing wealth gap between White and Black families, we do not have the luxury to compete against one another. The focus should be on teamwork.

Compete or Complete

Not all will start life with the tools to be successful. Manpower and teamwork can make up for a lack in resources or capital. The idea of focusing on "me and mines" or just on the growth of only your immediate family are ideologies that will weaken the community.

Let's say two separate Black business owners own separate food restaurants, does that mean they have to be in competition with each other? No, not necessarily. Just because the two business owners run businesses that are similar doesn't mean they have to compete with one another. For restaurant businesses in general, no one is going to eat at the same place every day at all hours of the day. Like most food establishments the two will probably end up sharing customers by default by way of variety.

The two business owners can help each other make more money and team up to do business ventures together that can be equally beneficial. For example, the two restaurants can come together to make events where both sides prosper. They can come together to do festivals, cater events, community functions, and even feed the homeless during holidays like Thanksgiving. Black people have to be realistic about their standing in this world.

Suffering from past and present-day systematic oppression that we all collectively share, competing against one another compounds the negative effects that oppression has on the group. Imagine living in a world where you feel like the world is against you, only to feel like the people who look like you are also against you.

The Culture That Was Created For Us

Black people presently and historic have had cities and towns of prominence. One of the most significant is "Black Wall Street" in Tulsa Oklahoma in the 1920's. However, like "Black Wall Street" efforts made by White oppressors to destroy the city by bombing the buildings the residents worked hard to build up. Now with certain laws in place and changes with the times, more subtle tactics are used to decay a city from within. Means like allowing for hard drugs to flood Black neighborhoods. This along with poverty and a lack of resources, can cause Black people to compete against one another.

We will never be allies to one another when we see each other as enemies. For my Black men who grew up in the streets or gang culture, you are being asked to let your old ideology go. Not all of the ideology of the culture is asked to be forgotten, just the part that makes you see another Black man as an enemy, a person you cannot trust, or someone you have to be in competition against.

It may be hard to let the past go, but its for the greater good of the community and its good to do for yourself. When you are inviting, more opportunities seem to come your way via the people you meet. Separate your enemies of the past from the Black people you meet today. Nothing is wrong with being vigilant, however you do not want to create a barrier between you and your people.

Root Each Other On:

When you become secure within yourself, you will know who you are, what you have to offer, and think in terms that you will be successful in due time. You will not hate the success of others. In fact you will be happy to see anyone succeed, but you will be especially happy to see someone who looks like you win. Especially if you belong to a group of people who have been oppressed or marginalized. Someone who is lacking in self-esteem has a higher likelihood to become jealous or envious when others are successful.

They may look at the situation like *"How come he or she got that before me?"* The truth is most of us aren't there to see the work people put in behind the scenes. Most of the time we see the end results of the work others put in. When you see others succeed you should be happy because it confirms that the same possibilities can be in store for you. Another person's success does not devalue you because they got "there" or became successful before you. We live in a world of abundance. Someone else's success does not take anything away from you.

Everyone will have their time of success and time of failure and what matters most is the type of person you are and character you display regardless of which you are currently dealing with. If we as humans deal with both success and failure alike, we should be less judgmental and more positive when people are dealing with either of the two circumstances. You should treat others how you would want to be treated when dealing with success or failure. Black people should be supportive of each other in times of success and failure.

The race collectively should always be especially supportive when other Black people succeed because of the past oppression we all share and the obstacles we deal with today. In my opinion this world for the most part is not formed for Black people to succeed ideally. When a Black person becomes successful, we should all be behind them.

A win for one of us is a win for all of us

collectively. When your time comes and all your hard work, knowledge, and efforts pay off do you want people to cheer for you or do you want them to downplay your success? The type of praise you give will be returned to you in due time. We live in a world of abundance where many can be successful if they're willing to gain the knowledge and put in the work.

Remember, Black people collectively have been in slavery longer than being free. Not all Black ancestors came to America as slaves, but they nonetheless had to endure a hard life in a country of racial oppression that is far worse than what we go through today. For that reason alone, anyone who is Black should cheer with enthusiasm when another Black person succeeds.

"But what if I don't like him/her?"

Let's be honest, we aren't all going to get along and that's just the truth. Some people may base their reality around characteristics that are flawed or have ways that don't fit with you. Or perhaps its someone you don't get along with or they did something you don't agree with. Distancing yourself from certain people is completely understandable. So, should you still root for Black people you don't like when they succeed? For me as long as the person's work does not harm the Black community, I can want a person to still be successful even if I do not care for the person.

Theirs a couple of Black people I can think of that I'd rather not deal with again. Let me be clearer, theirs some Black people that I do NOT like. That does not mean I want to see them fail. Even the people I don't like personally and public figures I don't like personally, I still want to see them succeed just because of our shared oppression.

That person you don't like may have a Black daughter or son who will be carrying us into the future as a people. It's better that our youth grow up in the best possible conditions even if they are the child of someone we don't like. We also must remember that people grow and evolve over time. Everyone that you idolize had to grow and mature into the person the world sees today. The person who has characteristic flaws that you simply can't tolerate may grow out of the ways you don't like.

We all have to remember that a lot of us Black people will come up in circumstance where we aren't fully nurtured. Some of us may have grew up around people who lacked high character and or integrity. Some may take longer to grow than others.

Black people globally already have enough obstacles to overcome and deal with in our life's experience. The last thing the collective needs is not to embrace each other's success. You never know the amount of work someone has put in. Trust and believe that the world most of the time gives people what they've earned or deserve.

If you had an honest conversation with most of the people you don't like, their past and their struggles, you would probably better understand them. If you both talked out the issues you have with each other, you may resolve the issue(s) you have with each other or at least come to an understanding. Most of the people we have issues with as humans can be resolved over an honest conversation.

Setting Standards: Unforgivable Offenses

We should root for Black people as much as possible, however we should not condone deviant behavior. There's a difference between giving grace for one to grow and pacifying toxic behavior. We should not root for those who steal from others. We should also be wary of those who try to conspire for one segment of Black people to clash with another segment of the population, for example, Black men vs Black women. We should not root for those that sell out, misrepresent, or turn their backs on the community. Some offense can be resolved and forgive. We do not root for people who harm children, men who hit women, and those who kill other than self-defense.

Celebrate Our Victories

Don't be a hater. When you see other Black people win whether you know them or not, feel good for them and be happy for their accomplishment. Don't try to diminish their success in the hopes of making yourself look or feel better.

Jealousy is unnecessary because if you work hard at your craft and make the right moves you too will have your days of victory. A good idea is to get to a place where the community can do business with each other and be successful together. We have to remember every time we separate ourselves, we make it easier for the entire community to be attacked. One person's actions alone won't take Black people to better places, its going to take a collective effort of an entire community.

Separatism:

The idea of colorism or judging one based on skin tone is an ideology that is not taken up by as many Black people in the past but still is prevalent among some Black people even in today. The thought that one's skin tone as in shade of darkness (from dark to light) was a determining factor in one's character, value, and beauty, is an issue worth addressing even if the concept does not dwell among society with the same vigor.

In the earlier 20th century, a mass variety of immigrants came to America for better opportunities only to be considered 2nd class citizens in preference to American born White men in society. These immigrants of non-Black ethnicity could better take the injustices they faced when told *"well at least you aren't Black!"* or were given rhetoric to make Black people to seem to be their enemy or someone who is going to take something from them. This has made African American's easily shunned and thought of as inferior when in comparison to any other race. African American's became the race that *"2nd class"* could look down on to feel superior.

African Americans for the most part never caused any real harm to most foreign people, communities, or places of origin, yet are shunned. African American's do not deserve such treatment however for Black people to apply the same logic to their own race is an idiotic practice.

During times of slavery those who were multiracial or those who were Black but had fairer skin received better treatment and were thought of in preference than Black people of darker skin. For whatever reason, such sentiments are shared worldwide; dark is beautiful, light is ugly."

Dark Skin vs Light Skin-

During slavery in America the Willie Lynch theory was "said" to be put into action. Here was the objective of theory:

> *"Keep the negro separated from light to dark and you will control them for the next 110 years."*

Whether Willie Lynch or the theory associate with his name really existed is an object for debate among historians. However, whether the theory or practice is true or not, such a theory is harmful to the Black community. Sadly, some in the Black community buy into this doctrine as they show preference towards other Black people based on skin tone. If you can get a community to see each other as an enemy, they will indeed be easier to control.

Some Black people buy into the ideas of the "Willie Lynch Theory" and make superficial judgments on each other based on skin tone. Such an ideology has lingered so long that stereotypes have emerged for light skin and dark skin people.

My Experience

Being of a brown skin tone I personally did not face any ridicule or prejudice specific to my skin tone, but I would hear the opinions of other Black people in reference to each other. One of the big ideas that sadly gained traction in the Black community for a while, is the idea that dark skin Black women are not as attractive as light skin Black women. Sad to say I know of Black men who have a dating preference based on skin tone before more meaningful features. Theirs even a stereotype that light skinned men are soft, pretty boys, or even feminine.

The light skin slave was more likely to work in the house which was work in better conditions and treatment among the slave master and their family. This caused resentment towards light skin Black people in the minds of some dark skin Black people. Even though such sentiments on the topic presently is usually used in a joking matter amongst men, we have to make sure it never becomes more than that, a harmless joke.

For quite some time an internal back and forth has been taking place among African Americans. Admittedly I don't see as many Black people following such practices as much anymore, sadly every now and then I hear tone preferential statements from Black people in reference to skin tone.

Dark skin women still deal with being thought of as less desirable among some Black men from a serious standpoint. Nothing's wrong with having a dating preference, however, a Black man should never think of a dark skin woman as being less beautiful, even if he exclusively dates light skin women. According to science the oldest human body was a dark skin woman. Most of our ancestors were dark skin women, to hate them is to hate ourselves.

Culture-ism: International Blacks vs African Americans

What's worse than "colorism is "culture-ism" among international Black people and African Americans. The negative stereotypes of African Americans is so strong that many people coming from international places are introduced to the stereotype before meeting an actual African American. Many people traveling from distant lands can have the idea of African Americans as being "ghetto", "ill mannered" or "inferior." Some African Americans may see Black foreigners as poor, and a punching bag for ridicule just for being from a different place of origin.

This barrier that exists among some international Black people and African Americans works against the Black community as a whole (which they both belong to) and works in the interest of our oppressors. Some may make the mistake of judging an entire group based off a few acquaintances.

When both people are oppressed either historically or presently by the same systems, it makes no sense to devalue each other. Separating each other is comparable to soldiers of the same unit shooting at each other while enemies advance on the both of them. African Americans and Black internationals need to work together to empower and help each other's visions come true. The two factions may feel like they are fighting different battles but may not know that they both have common enemies in certain aspects.

African Americans and international Blacks both have different perspectives, knowledge on business, and can be an asset to one another. Hard times are always better endured and easier to overcome when you have someone going through it with you. African Americans and Black people from different countries of origin can gain a great deal from each other, but we have to be able to at least be able to smile and say "hello" to one another. So much can be accomplished when we see each other as allies and not enemies or someone to feel indifferent about. Imagine Black people across the globe as one force, solving each other's injustices and coming up with solutions to all their problems.

- Gain an understanding where you find beauty and value in Black people of all skin shades from dark to light.

- Do not engage in rhetoric that promotes the idea of someone being ugly or attaching stereotypes based on someone's skin tone.

- Raise your children, the younger people in your family, and the youth you interact with to value people of light and dark skin tones.

- Defend dark skin women.

- Tell young dark skin women that they are beautiful.

- Do NOT say the following: *"You are beautiful, for a dark skin girl."* This is not a compliment. If you are a dark skin woman such a phrase should not be taken as a compliment.

- Be open to greeting and engage in conversation with a Black person from a different place of origin.

- Learn the lifestyles, cultures, and issues facing other Black people around the world.

- Follow Black news outlets from different countries on social media to be kept up to date on international affairs.

- Compliment others as much as possible including complete strangers.

- No more mean mugs when making eye contact.

WE WILL NOT JUDGE EACH OTHER BASED ON RELIGION

People in general tend to be fanatical about their religious beliefs. To the credit of Black people who believe any religions of the world, these beliefs give Black people hope for a better tomorrow and afterlife. Religion for some has given them a path, a purpose, guidance, and a reason for being in service to others. Even though religions have made some better, they have also made some judgmental and close-minded, even towards their own people.

Personally, I respect all religions under the sun, however I do not condone religious practices of any kind that promote the hatred or the devaluing of people who do not practice the same religion. No offense is intended here but no matter what religion you believe in, you were Black first. Before you had any knowledge of any religion. The bond between you and other Black people should NOT be broken because of your choice of religion.

"People of other races practice religions separatism just like Black people, so what's the issue?"

People of any African heritage or people of dark complexion do not have the luxury to discriminate against each other based on religion. Most of us believe in the religions that were taught to us. Some subconsciously pick a religion for social acceptance, while consciously follow none of the practices of that religion or do so in a partial manner.

Regardless of the depth of your religious

beliefs, your ties to your brothers and sisters in oppression should always be greater. Your strongest allegiance should belong to those who are fighting the same struggle you endure. According to science, Black people have existed long before any modern-day religion.

The previous text is not meant to demean the religions of the world. The path that others take is their concern and none of your business. According to most religions you will be solely judged on your life by the creator you believe in. You should mostly concern yourself with your own spiritual journey and let other people be concerned with theirs. I believe that religions are supposed to unite people, not divide them.

Always remember there's multiple reasons to love someone one or care for someone, religious belief is just one of many facets to consider when interacting with someone. You don't have to agree on the same religion in order to work with each other and see value in each other. Also remember in past times of Jim Crow and the Civil Rights Movement that Black people of all religions were equally discriminated against.

If a group of people are collectively damaged by racial discrimination, then it only makes sense for this same race of people to stick together and help one. What we should not to do is create a barrier among one of us based on religion.

If a person is truly confident in their way of life, then that person should not need the validation of others, or a need to convert everyone to their beliefs. True confidence comes when you believe what you want and care less of what others think of your choice and beliefs.

"Any Black person who still believes in God or religion is a fool.."

Judgement From the Non-Religious

I cannot stand religious people who push their faith on others and judge those who think differently than them. Ironically enough I see atheist doing the exact same thing; judging Christian's and other religious people because of their beliefs. It's so annoying to have someone project their belief on you while totally ignoring how you were raised and what you believe.

Some atheists I know act as if they are annoyed at just the mention of religion from others. If one is imposing their beliefs on another, annoyance I can understand, but some act irritated with the just the mention of religion. For an atheist to be concerned about what a religious person believes, turns them in to exact person they despise. When we truly love each other, we can see each other's differences and respect each other even if we don't agree.

One reason why I have love and respect the Nation of Islam because Black people benefit from their teachings and actions, even if they are not Muslim. The truth is there's valid points on both ends of the spectrum, the religious and the atheist point of view. Breaking this barrier will do great things for the community. Other races may struggle with the concept of religious and non-religious people loving each other, as Black people we do not have the luxury to be divided on this issue. We can do powerful things when we love each other despite our differences.

Loving Each Other

Having love for each other has to be your first religion, no matter what you believe. Of course, religions have brought people together in a loving way. Religion historically has also been used to oppress others, divide people, wage war on other societies, and have eradicated the cultural practices of others.

People in general have to always remember that religion has played a role in both the salvation and the destruction of others. What this means is religion within itself is usually not "good" or "bad" but at the mercy of how the people use it. How will you use religion? Will you use it to condemn others or to love and help others?

What you should be concerned about is the character, attitude, and actions of a person and how the religion they practice influences them. It doesn't matter if someone is a devout Christian if they are molesting children. If an atheist saves the life of others, should we be concerned about who they are praying to? In my opinion, actions and character means a lot more than sharing the same religion.

- Understand that your religious practice is yours. What someone else decides to believe has nothing to do with you.

- Learn how to value people who think totally opposite of you.

- Learn how NOT to take what others believe or say about your religion personally.

- Learn how to be confident in your beliefs. You do not need others to believe what you believe.

- Concern yourself more with the actions one does instead of what they believe.

- Understand that solutions for the community are bigger than believing in the same religion.

- Religion can be just as important as the love for your people, it should NOT be more important.

- Put your differences aside and come up with solutions together.

WE WILL NOT JUDGE EACH OTHER BASED ON SOCIAL STATUS

When statistics are presented about virtually anything, Black people seem always to be the race that struggles with everything. Many Black people fail to see worth in self so they need material things to give them worth. This is why studies show that Black people are more loyal to brand names more than any other race. Why? Because Black people are usually attracted to brand names that will make them seem more valuable in their own eyes and in the eyes of others.

Black people have more spending power collectively than many countries around the world, yet unfortunately a good portion of that money is spent on material possessions usually from non-Black businesses.

Black people are finding their false sense of worth in designer shoes, purses, fancy cars, and clothes. What's even worse is in many occasions these things that some buy to find their worth, they can't afford to buy based on their income. The thirst to be "worthy" is so strong that many will buy things that will actually drain their monetary value. A lot of the popular things that Black people will spend money on are liabilities that will take spending power from them and in some cases these liabilities can become a money pit.

Social Status

Some of us check to see what type of shoes, clothes, and car one drives in order gauge the worth of someone. In the eyes of some Black people what you buy is more important than your character and values as a person.

Be warned, no one on Earth can buy their

personal worth or self esteem. If your worth can be bought it can also be sold. You may run the risk of being manipulated and pimped by people who have long money. One runs a bigger risk of being a "sell out" when their worth can be bought instead of instilled inside of them. A righteous person and a corrupt person can buy the same exact items, so looking for worth in material things is fools' gold.

True confidence is present before you put anything on or use any material possession. A woman or man who has true confidence has strong self worth regardless of the brand of shoes he or she has on. Martin Luther King said: *"Judge a man not by the color of his skin but the content of their character."* Although this message may have been intended to address racism, however if we replace the word *"color of skin"* with *"material possessions"* the same point is made.

One's character and values cannot be determined by their outfit. Be not concerned with what a person can buy, instead concern yourself with a person's character, morals, how they treat their family, work ethic, goals, ideas, manners, generosity, and attitude. Concern yourself with what a person does for their own community and people.

When more in the community can see worth in self before buying anything they can resist the temptation to buy liabilities and focus on buying assets which can bring in more money instead of just looking the part.

We Are Worth More Than What We Can Buy:

Black people have the global stigma and stereotype of being poor or bad with money. Many of the race know this so they use this thought to prove value, by buying things to show that they have money or status. Many Black people are out to prove they are not poor and valuable, however if your value in self is solely materialistic it can cause you to devalue yourself and others when you don't have certain things.

"But aren't I entitled to have nice things in life?"

There's no doubt that there *is* some value in some of the things we have and our appearance does matter, but it should not be the most important part of your being. Sometimes it's helpful to dress in terms of the person you want to become. It's good to look nice and presentable. It can be beneficial in business depending upon the situation. You only live once and it's good to treat yourself from time to time with good things.

I like the concept of Black people owning nice things, it becomes an issue however when we judge others for not having the same things. Besides judging each other, placing too much value on material things can hurt one financially. One can desire material items to the point where they put off priorities, or the purchase or assets all to buy material things which more than likely will be liabilities.

Getting What You Want vs Getting What You Need

No matter what your circumstances are your priorities should always be taken care of first before spending on any of your wants. Luxury items are exactly as they are said to be, items of *luxury.* These items should only be purchased when you are in a state of luxury. Nothings worse than seeing a Black person who only looks or seems like they live in luxury and not have it in reality.

If you are still finding your path in life you are better off spending your money on things that will make you more money, also known as ***assets,*** so you can buy the things you want with ease. Even those who have a lot of money should still have some type of limit on luxury because for the most part luxury items just have a popular brand name behind them, but do not always enhance you. Even items or goods that are luxury that you can afford should be looked at as something that adds to you, but it does not make you into the person you are. You should have the same confidence in yourself whether you have luxury items or not.

A good majority of luxury items are produced by companies that are not owned by Black people, whom of which will probably do nothing beneficial for the community. In fact, rumor has it that many of the luxury brands Black people praise don't want Black people buying or promoting their brands. How and where we spend our money is very important. You should be very intentional with whom you spend your money with. If you value your community, make sure your money has a positive impact on the community.

If you want to buy things (even liabilities) at least buy from a Black business so that Black people can reap the benefits of the money you are willing to spend. When we become more intentional with where and whom we spend our money with we will ask questions like: "Who am I supporting with my money?" Or "Will spending here benefit my people?"

There's always someone else who has more money or material things than you; does that alone make them better than you? No, not at all. Sure, this person may understand and maintain money better than you but that is just one facet of existence. Therefore no one should judge anyone because there will always be someone who has more than you. You have to ask yourself what is the value of your respect if it can just be brought? Theirs many people who live with poor character and principals, but they have a lot of money and things.

Beautiful Death:

Some want to impress others so bad that they will kill themselves financially to do so. Some may even go so extreme to damage themselves in other areas of life so they can have things that are liabilities. They will have nice things and look successful on the outside, while the rest of their life is in chaos because of such behavior, hence the saying "beautiful death".

In a capitalistic society money and status is culturally put on a pedal stool above all. This means that a lot of people will act like they have more money than they actually have. They will take on car notes that they cannot afford, they will take on mortgages that they cannot afford, and buy clothes that are way beyond their budget. They live grand on the outside while they are dying on the inside.

I had a good friend who had a job taking pictures of houses in foreclosure or facing eviction. She was surprised to see how many houses had residents that had 3-4 fancy cars with big and beautiful homes but facing foreclosure. She said if those houses weren't on her list, she would have never known they were in foreclosure. Some of the houses looked like mansions and you would have thought they were rich from the outside looking in.

What you do in one area of your life shows up in other areas of your life. If you are willing to sacrifice your money for the sake of others, what about your health, success, and happiness? If you have to sacrifice such things for a person's approval, then you are trying to please the wrong people.

Stunt Culture

Some people who have luxury brand items may show them off to inspire others into thinking they can have the same thing, which is to be commended! I love to see Black people have nice things whether it's a good pair of shoes or a nice car. However, theirs many Black people who will show off what they have because they feel they are better than someone else who does not have the same things. Unfortunately, theirs many Black people who do this to each other, they *stunt* on each other.

In many instances in rap culture and in everyday life of Black people, one of the norms many of us have collectively accepted is to ridicule other Black people who don't have the same value of things from a material standpoint. As said earlier, in the early 1900's immigrants and foreigners faced prejudice in America but the rhetoric they were given is that they were better than Black people even though they weren't equal to Whites.

Such an ideology worked as many immigrants and foreigners looked down on Black people and think less of them in stature even if Black people never wronged them. This is one of many reasons why some foreigners and people of other races (non-White) look down on Black people as if they are not good enough. Black people have taken the same ideology and applied it to poor Black people or even just Black people who are not flashy with their money. For the foreigners it was:

"I may not be White but at least I'm not Black."

Too many Black people adopted the same ideology; "I may be Black but at least I'm not poor *and* Black."

In present times a good population of Black people feel like their peers in the community are worth nothing unless they have money or flashy luxury items. When someone Black adopts this way of thinking, they are thinking with the minds of their oppressor. Joking around and judging someone based off of what they have are two different things. Joking with each other is a part of Black culture. We must make sure there's a clear difference between joking and hatred.

Black people must be able to see value in each other regardless of what they have. Always remember that Black people have made tremendous things out of nothing, and from an individual standpoint many have become successful starting from humble beginnings. Many Black people are of value but maybe they aren't in their season of success yet. We should be a race of people who give each other the benefit of the doubt more often than not.

You have to remember all of us humans will deal with ups and downs. Make sure you treat people in accordance with how you want to be treated no matter what end of the spectrum they are currently on. If you are Black, you have enough enemies in this world, do not strive to make more because you don't like the way someone else spends their money.

A person's talents, skills, and knowledge should be held in higher regard than the things they can buy. Most material things will do nothing but depreciate for as long as you have them, however ones skills, talents, and knowledge can be useful in bad and good times. In the hands of the right person can be beneficial for a lifetime. The things we should be most impressed about each other are the things that are already built inside of us.

Money Means Something, But Not Everything

There's power in having good finances no doubt but it does not completely define anyone. Be less concerned with the amount of money people have and more concerned with what they do with their money. A man or woman can be rich and have a lot of money but what does it all mean if these people with money are not using their resources to be an asset to others?

The unfortunate truth is that too many Black people want to become rich and wealthy so they can provide for *their* people only. When I say *"their"* people, I do not mean the Black community but one's family and friends only. Instead of using their resources to be helpful to the community, some would rather use their wealth to look down on other Black people. We hear it in our music and our culture, where Black people are in a monetary arms race for status against one another.

"I don't owe nobody else nothing! All I need to worry about is my friends and family and that's it!"

This has been said multiple times in the book, but the redundancy is done purposely to drive the point home; **WE DO NOT HAVE THE SAME LUXURY AS EVERYONE ELSE.** No other race on earth has been through the trauma and oppression Black people have without reparations. What type of world would we be living in if Martin Luther King Jr only worried about his family only? Where would Black people be if Malcolm X, Angela Davis, Huey P. Newton, Stokely Carmichael, and Fred Hampton, only cared to fight for their family and friends only, ignoring the issues Black people had to deal with? If Harriet Tubman and Fredrick Douglass only focused on themselves and their families many Black people would have remained enslaved. In fact, without these two theirs a good chance that the force to abolish slavery would not have been as vigorous. We would be living in even worse times than we find ourselves in now if these people had a *"me and mines only"* attitude. These people risked their reputation, their freedom, and for some their lives.

These people did not have to risk anything for any of us, but they chose to. They could have just stayed home and worried only about their family. Some of these people would still be alive today if they did not stand against the injustices we faced, however where would we be as people if these activists did not make a stand? Its sad that these people sacrificed so much for us all, while in modern times some Black people are afraid to sacrifice money for the greater good of the people.

What a person does with their money gives you some insight into where their mindset is and what is important to them. Who cares about what type of car a person drives if they aren't an asset to the community they are a part of. If a Black person is wealthy but doesn't invest in their own people, that can give you some indication of what type of person they would be if they were living in times of slavery, Jim Crow and the Civil Rights Movement. They would be focused on their lives only and could care less about the rest of us. This is why looking for a person's character, goals, and morals, will give you a better indication of who this person is rather than judging them based off their income.

Seeing The Bad In A "Good" Status-

In the community judgment based off of social status goes both ways where one can be marginalized by what they don't have however, there's also a concept within society where some who have good social statuses are not accepted. While some may judge someone on their economic status in a positive way, some may judge others negatively based on apparent high social status.

The opposite of gaining value in one's eyes for what they have is having envy, jealousy, and disdain for what another person has accomplished. There's a negative concept that one is *"soft"* if they did not grow up in the *"hood"*, *"ghetto"*, urban area, or ran down neighborhood. For some the idea of being Black means coming from poverty or being ghetto.

Many think with the mindset that one is not *"real"* if they did not grow up in the hood. Even people of other races think this way. This sediment is highly believed in especially among Black youth. If every Black person's goal is to be successful, shouldn't we look at it as a good thing when one of us does not have to grow up in poverty or in a rough neighborhood?

Do we as Black people have to buy into the idea that you must be *"hood"* or from the hood to be *"really"* Black? Although circumstances and environment help mold us, judging a person by where they are from alone, is just as idiotic as judging a person on race alone. No one can help where they are born and the circumstances we were born into. Shame on any Black person that made another Black person from an affluent background guilty about their upbringing.

From my experience this can and has cause many Black youngsters from affluent neighborhoods and from middle to upper class, to act out negatively. The case for some of these youth is they may act bad to prove how *"hard"* they are and may even try to be *"hood"*. Being *"hood"* by many in Black culture is celebrated while being from affluence is looked down on.

In many cases the community looks down on those who lie about the circumstance they come from, but if we choose to keep buying into this ideology that you are only as Black as the hood you are from, can we blame youngsters who pose as gangster, and thugs when that's what a lot of us respect? How is being *hood* helpful for the Black community?

Let's make this clear, your value as a Black person does not depend on how ghetto you are. Your value is determined by your actions and character, regardless of where you are from.

If you are too affluent some may even resort to

calling you *"White"* no matter how dark your skin is, or what your family and ancestors have been through. This is another negative idea that needs to be done away with. We can't be a community of people who hates to see others "make it" and mock them for the success they were able to accumulate. We should be happy when anyone who looks like us achieves success, and their children are able to start off in better circumstances because of it.

Just because someone is from the suburbs doesn't mean they are *"soft"* or prefer to be White. Not every Black person from the hood is "tough", a hustler, and a representation for all Black people. We as people must not let society fit us into this one mold of *"how a Black person is supposed to be."* If anything, Black people from the hood and affluent settings should work together to do bigger and better things. We should be respecting each other's differences not using them to separate.

We have the freedom to be a diverse people with a variety of interests not this general perception society has for us. We are free to be interested in things normally associate with Black people and we also have the right to be interested in things outside of what is "normal" for black people to be into.

A Black person from the suburbs can be strong, tough, a hustler, and still have a strong sense of Black pride. The reason why we as Black people need to focus on one's personality, character, morals, and goals because things like where one is from, what car do they drive, and how much money they have will fool us every time.

Measure Character, Morals, and Goals-

If you must measure a person at least focus on personality traits and not superficial means. If you look deeper to see someone for who they truly are, you will find the truth about this person. A person of strong character, morals, and goals is an asset to your life no matter how much money have presently.

Some of the best of us who have made the world a better place for Black people to live for weren't rich people. Martin Luther King and Malcom X were not rich people. They weren't even driven by money (as far as I know). Are these people less valuable because they weren't driven by money? Some of our biggest stars in the entertainment community use their wealth for a good cause for Black individuals, yet most of our stars do very little for Black communities while in some cases having the resources to do so. Before you down the next poor person you see, remember the activist who was not rich but risked everything for their people.

Some people from the hood use their struggle to their advantage, while others are scum to it. Some people born in affluent neighborhoods use their advantage to get ahead in life and be helpful to others. While some from this same setting may become entitled, soft, lazy, and ignorant to the struggles of their own people. The point is we are all different and are going to have different individual reactions to the environments, the things we have, and our ways of life.

If you were to take someone with high morals, strong characteristics, goals, and work ethic, they will prevail no matter what setting they are in or what they have. The same is true on the negative end of the spectrum. One can have a lot, but what does it mean if their own people or community do not benefit from their wealth.

Why do we look down on Black people born in affluent settings when the goal of many is to provide a better life than the ones we had growing up? Why do we need to judge each other so hastily at all? Instead of worrying about the superficial ideas of worth that stereotypical Black culture embraces, we can establish our own standard.

- Have the mentality of greeting the janitor of a company with the same respect you would show the CEO.

- Do NOT judge people based off the material possession that they do or do NOT have.

- Be more concerned with one's actions and character and be less concerned about what they have or where they are from.

- Understand that a proper speaking Black person from an affluent background should be valued and is still apart of the community.

- Learn to respect the differences we all have.

- Do NOT make people feel as if they have to prove their "Blackness" to you.

- Money is a tool; it alone should NOT be a factor in determining one's worth.

- If you made someone feel less valuable because of what they do or do NOT have, take the time to apologize to that person.

- Understand that you are valuable because of what's inside you.

- Nothings wrong with buying nice things. Just make sure you can afford it and understand that what you buy alone does not define you.

- Understand the difference between an asset (something that makes you money) and a liability (something that cost you money).

- Realize that you do not live for the approval of others. The opposite is also true however, others do not live for your approval.

- Always prioritize your spending. Spend on necessities first and you can spend on less needed things thereafter. Understand the difference between what you want and what you need.

- Do NOT put yourself in financial ruin for the sake of others.

- Do NOT engage in rhetoric with others who judge people based off of the material things they have.

WE WILL BE SELF RELIAINT

I believe that after slavery Black people collectively are looking to be saved by something or someone else. No doubt theirs been plenty of stories of Black men and women who created their own means of business, making money, maintaining health, and living life on their own. Yet if we are talking about Black people in the collective from a macro standpoint many of us are waiting for someone or something to make conditions better for us in the United States and globally.

Author Carter G. Woodson makes a profound statement on the issue in ***The Miseducation of the Negro***:

> *"History shows that it does not matter who is in power or what revolutionary forces take over the government, those who have not learned to do for themselves and have to depend solely on others never obtain any more rights or privileges than they had in the beginning."*

The statement above applies to all people in general, he goes on to speak specifically to Black people:

> *"...we see again the tendency of the Negro to look to some force from without to do for him what he must learn to do for himself (herself)."*

A LONG History of Mistrust

Many Black people think the United States government will save them. They believe that if they vote on the right causes in masses, have more representatives that look like them, and or protest our grievances to higher authorities for the change we all mostly want to see transpire in our lives. The reality is many promises made to Black people in the past that have went un-honored.

Buffalo soldiers (fierce and legendary black soldiers who fought for American interest during America's post-colonial period) were told by a general who later became president (and well-known racist) Andrew Jackson that they would be granted freedom if they sacked a Native American tribe for him. The soldiers carried out their orders perfectly only to realize they were lied to and were not granted the freedom that they were told they would have.

After the Civil War black generals were asked by Abraham Lincoln what it would take for Black people to succeed thus forward and the Black generals unanimously came up with the idea of "40 acres and a mule." Owning land is one of the most beneficial things one can own and a true sign of prosperity. Those who have their own land can become self sufficient. Unfortunately, in President Abraham Lincoln was assassinated before he could make good on that promise.

The next president to take office was racist Andrew Johnson who made sure that Black people would not get what they asked for. In cruel irony, slave owners actually got reparations after the American Civil War, where Black people were free, but bewildered, uneducated, and unfairly thrusted out into an unfamiliar world. In fact, Black people would become targets in the Reconstruction area of the south as it was told that they were mostly responsible for the hardships the south faced after the war.

During *The Great Depression* Franklin D. Roosevelt came up with *"The New Deal"* which was a constructive project that would give the middle-class jobs and benefits and usher the nation out of The Great Depression. The catch is Black people got very little out of this deal. Most of the jobs and opportunities went to the White middle class.

When affluent Black business owners formed Black Wall Street in Tulsa, Oklahoma, they were bombed by White citizens from nearby cities out of shear jealousy and nothing more. The United States Government did nothing to bring the people who bombed the city to justice. The United States has recognized and honored the survivors of the tragedy in Tulsa Oklahoma, but as far as monetary compensation gave nothing.

During The Civil Rights Era of American history many Black neighborhoods were lynched by the KKK, the US government did little to stop such things from happening. A Black person could actually go to jail for defending themselves against a White person or worse during those times.

At this time the US seemed more concerned about the wellbeing of people in other countries like Korea and Vietnam because of the political interest of those places. The FBI during the Civil Rights era and prior to played an active role in dismantling Black civil rights efforts and leaders.

Almost all of which who've rose to have a strong voice for the injustices Black people both historically and presently deal with, have been investigated, harassed, or dismantled all together. Leaders like Malcom X, Martin Luther King Jr, and the organization the Black Panthers were investigated by the FBI. The Black Panthers was an organization about community defense, education, and community engagement. Such organizations were destroyed from the inside out by the FBI.

In the late 1980's-1990's it was uncovered that many US agencies allowed for crack cocaine to be sold in Black neighborhoods exclusively to fund the side of the Nicaraguan war that the US wanted to win during the country's civil war.

Even during The Recession many Black families were hit harder because the sub-prime loans offered to them had higher interest rates with volatile terms their white counterparts with the same credit score (or lower) were not offered the same loans.

As of now (2023) the wealth gap is 100,000 for Whites and about 18,000 for Blacks. Even with such a disparity between the numbers and a long-standing history of systemic oppression Black people have yet to receive reparations, and when the issue is bought up by those in government their always seem to be some "obstacle" that makes it hard for them to determine how and when reparations should be paid. Some believe that Black people should not be paid reparations at all.

Native Americans were given reparations (which they deserved), Japanese American's were given reparations for being held in internment camps during World War II, which once again they deserved. It can be insensitive to compare one groups oppression to another but if these racial groups got reparations for their grief, surely Black people deserve reparations too.

If a nation does not honor a people whom of which have helped them win wars throughout the country's history, I wonder what makes Black people think that the United States government would ever do anything that is in the best interest of Black people? I know some Black people who may be beaming with patriotism who make take issue with what I have previously stated, however all that is mentioned above is true. The previous paragraphs are not to inspire the community in America to go against their country, however truths must be told of the nation's relationship towards the race.

Voting, protesting, and taking seats in government positions, are some things that may be beneficial to Black people, however one should not put all their eggs in the basket of asking the government to give us the treatment we deserve. Even in the corporate world Black people make demands to corporations we don't own when disrespected. We demand that businesses not owned by one of our own treats us fairly and do the things we want.

Even when it comes to religion many Black people are hoping to be saved by the work of a godly being, or being rewarded in heaven when they are dead. Most Black churches do little for the communities they are located in. At face value most are a place where you can hear good rhetoric, give the pastor a pay day, and benefit only the congregation of the church. However, I see very few churches do functions for the community (outside their congregation).

Sometimes we may even think that other groups that are marginalized or thought of as a minority in this country are in the same fight with us to topple oppressive systematic racism and oppression. However, that may be wishful thinking. Some Asian, Hispanic, Indian, Arab, and immigrants of all kinds may stand with us in solidarity against oppressive systems but not ALL of them align with tearing down oppressive systems and ideas in society.

Some people from these racial groups identify more closely with European ideologies and look down on Black people. Some of the people from their countries of origin even promote the idea that lighter skin is preferred, and dark skin is ugly even among non-Black people.

Some of these people think of all the negative stereotypes about Black people are true. With many lacking a true account of Black history and how Black people have been oppressed, it gives some the idea that Black people are mostly responsible for their own oppression.

Has the US government done better for Black people compared to past conditions? Yes! Has religion given many Black people hope, a better way of living, and love for their fellow man/woman? Yes! Have many non-Black people of other races help Black people escape oppression, spoke out on the injustices, and marched with us during protest? YES!

The previous statements aren't to conspire you to go against your government, religion of choice, or against anyone who isn't Black. All 3 factors can be used to combat Black oppression. One can get involved in government politics, use religion to promote peace, and one can join forces with non-Black people to fight against oppression. We can use these factions to help us fight our oppression but Black people putting all their focus into just these areas of interest alone will not prevail in making a better life for the community.

You may not get the change you want at the time you want because you are asking others to make or help provide a better life for you and your people. No one will be more concerned about Black issues than Black people. Black people need to save themselves by coming together and establishing our own business, our own towns/neighborhoods (not *hoods*) and establish our own ideas and way of life. We may have allies who will fight alongside of us or support our causes however to be blunt, no one is coming to save Black people; we have to save ourselves.

Black Independence

In many instances when a Black person faces issues from businesses or organizations the first idea in mind is to state your grievances and demand better. Even though there's power in demanding fair treatment and equality, Black people in these situations usually find themselves in a position to make demands with no leverage. In some cases, time alone can eventually silence Black outcry on issues.

Even though the community should demand better treatment, in these situations Black people find themselves in the asking position. Whether it's a peaceful discussion, or a protest, it's all the same; Black people are **asking** for better conditions instead of providing it for themselves.

Carter G Woodson explained this concept perfectly in **"The Mis-Education of the Negro"**:

"Negros do not need someone to guide

them to what persons of another race have developed. They must be taught to think and develop something for themselves. It is most pathetic to see Negros begging others for a chance as we have been doing recently. "Do not force us into starvation" we said. Let us come into your stores and factories and do a part of what you are doing to profit by our trade."

The Negro as a slave developed this fatal sort of dependency; and, restricted mainly to menial service and drudgery during nominal freedom, he has not grown out of it. Now the Negro is facing the ordeal of either learning to do for himself (and herself) or to die out gradually in the bread line in the ghetto."

For Black people to be self-reliant we must be able to support ourselves with the basic necessities needed for survival. This means that members of the Black population need to be able to have their own land, grow/harvest their own food, provide energy resources, businesses, owned banks, hospitals, and a governing body to create, and execute laws. Theirs many Black people who will point out how hard it will be or how long it will take to collectively bring all these elements together in a successful manner. A toxic trait that some have is they find an issue with every solution concerning the community and they give in to the ideas that we are doomed to what others are giving or will allow.

A recurring theme in the community is an idea of being mostly focused on short-term goals instead of long-term goals. Yes, what was stated as necessities for Black independence seems impossible if you are thinking of accomplishing these things overnight. Achieving independence will not be accomplished easily, however it is something that we in the present owe to those who came before us and those who will come after us. The goal is to push the community into a better place than it was and is now.

It will take skilled individuals, teams, businesses, and groups of Black interest to come together and combine resources and create a self-reliant Black neighborhood, cities, or perhaps a county. Of course, none of us can do all these things by ourselves, however, more can be accomplished when skilled individuals or teams combine forces for the community's greater good. One person can own the land, another owns their own medical practice, another can own a utilities company. It will take a team effort of people with different skills but with the same common goal in mind.

Even if these ideas seem like a steep climb, we as a people must not give up hope that we can create and sustain a strong independent community. We must think of where we would still be as people if Harriet Tubman, Fredrick Douglass, or Booker T. Washington waited for someone else? What if they thought they were powerless and simply took what was given? To make and establish change you will have to take on risk and go outside your comfort zone. Even when facing a difficult task Black people cannot be afraid to go after a better way of life.

One can simply do their part by becoming a business owner or becoming skilled in an area of expertise that all people will need. Focus on skills essential to a community like, plumbing/ irrigation, being electrician, or HVAC. When you can provide a service that people need to survive, you recession proof your business, you increase income possibilities, and you become a valued asset to the community. You become a high value Black person when your work benefits you and the community around you.

Providing For Self

Providing for yourself goes far beyond making good money to pay bills and maintain your lifestyle. Providing for yourself may be more work, but the work provides you freedom. No one is telling you to quit your job. It's a good idea to have some sort of independence outside of your career and job. This allows you to better assist the community, gives you more flexibility, and gives you leverage when dealing with your career or job. Having other income options is better than being at the mercy of one job. Power comes when you are not restricted to what others offer. If you have options, you have leverage.

Money

If you lost your job today, would you be able to survive? Every Black person should have some form or means of income outside of a job working for another person. Not a part time job on the side, but a hustle or gig in which they are in complete control of the income and movement of the business.

It's a good idea to have their own means of income in case they are met with hostility on the job, work in unbearable environments, or hit their head on a glass ceiling.

"Not every Black person is built to be an

entrepreneur!"

Of course, entrepreneurship isn't for everyone. However, there's a difference between having another source of income and running a business. One could invest in a business opportunity with money, credit, or resources while doing very little or no work at all. Someone who is interested in investing in a company for equity may have to do their due diligence in researching the company.

Regardless of how it's done whether its owning your own company on the side, a side hustle, investing in the business of someone else, or even the stock market, every Black person has to make the conscious effort to have a hustle independent of a job or career. Those who do not have multiple streams of income may be more likely to put up with disrespect and anxiety on the job because they have no other options.

Many may think that simply getting another job will be better for them. In some cases, this may be true, however not everyone will deal with the same job market and job availability so a "better job" may or may not be available. Also, you find you have no time for yourself or the personal things you need to do. Take control of your livelihood or someone else will.

Industries-

Having self-reliant industries is imperative in building strong neighborhoods, towns, and communities. Whatever businesses, industries, items that exist in the world, a Black version is needed. This means we need Black leaders in tech industries, utilities, fashion/ clothing, manufacturing, construction, security, art, literature, entertainment, health/ medical, and food/agriculture. We cannot be a upwardly mobile people if we have to constantly go to others to gain resources in the areas of industry listed above.

Having such industries will allow us not to be trapped into whatever treatment, or deals presented to us because we have no other options. Not only are these industries vital for the survival of a town or city, but they will also provide a variety of jobs. Controlling the industry gives you power to create and maintain one's own economy.

A people who are not self-reliant after overcoming the horrors of bondage in some sense justify the old stereotypes which stated that Black people are too incompetent to be independent and will always need someone or something to provide for them. I get annoyed with Black people who make demands to companies that are not owned by Black people do right by Black people. It's understandable to ask for fair treatment from an organization however the same energy that can be put into protesting or making demands can be used to build our own companies and industries that are a service to our areas of concern and interest.

- Know and understand the history of how governing bodies in the United States have not only mistreated African Americans but have also dismantled Black independence and have not made good on past promises.

- Demanding better treatment from the United States government and the companies that operate in the nation is encouraged, however seek forms of independence where you are less reliant on the United Stated government and the businesses that operate within.

- If you have a career or job, create another form of income outside of that job. Create a business, side hustle, or investing in a business are better solutions than to get a 2nd job.

- Learn how to grow your own food. If you are a meat eater learn how to hunt.

- Create your own garden.

- If you are unsure what to do with your life or career, invest in a field that can be beneficial to your community. Some examples are; being an electrician or plumber. You can learn the trade and form a business around it.

- Understand their needs to be a Black version of every service and product in society. It does not matter if people of other races are "already doing it." We need a Black version of every aspect of life.

WE WILL HELP
EACH OTHER

For the community to be successful we have to be a race of people who are not only willing but enthusiastic to help another Black person. I'm not asking you to go beyond your means to where it can be harmful to you, but you just do what you can to help without overextending yourself.

If you see another Black person struggling with their car, go over and see if you can help them. If you know someone who needs a ride, provide them with a ride from time to time. Be a non-judgmental ear that someone can vent frustrations to. Be helpful to anyone regardless of race, but make sure to be especially helpful to a Black person in need if you have the means to help. When approaching strangers always ask them "Do you need some help?" In a world that is mainly working against the interest of Black people we must give a helping hand to each other.

Our children hold the key to the future, not just your biological children (if you have any) but other Black children are also your responsibility to a degree. Not in the sense of monitoring, or watching over, but always be helpful and inviting to young children and address them in a respectful manner. For children you do not personally know, your only goal is to make sure they are respected, and they are safe.

When you are among our youth, greet them, smile, or nod to let them know they are among people who respect and value them. We must be a people who are willing to look out for each other when we see another Black person in need, and not just people in our family or people we personally know.

Of course, there's a general barrier strangers put up against other strangers which is understandable, however we must be willing to put that aside when one of us is in need. Watching another like you fail or struggle should not be to your benefit either. We share a common struggle (from a macro standpoint) so should help each other, believe in each other, and cheer when victorious for anyone who is Black. Does this mean you can't do these such things for non-Black people? Of course not!

Helping anyone in need regardless of race is the right thing to do. Just make sure you especially do the things stated earlier for the community.

The Act of Being Helpful

Helping in time of crisis is of course encouraged. Be helpful to each other in smaller ways. We should be holding doors for each other when we see someone struggling to carry something. We should ask "do you need help?" or see if we can be of any assistance when we see one of our own in trouble. Black men should want to be gentlemen when in the presence of Black women, and our women shouldn't mind catering or being hospitable to a Black man.

Black elders should be respected and always checked on to see if they need assistance with anything. Unless actions and character tell you otherwise, Black elders should be held in the highest regard, for all of them have some value to those younger than them.

We must make sure we are not quick to judge and condemn our youth as many popular negative stereotypes about our youth are thought to be true by many. If you see a young Black person doing wrong and you feel inclined to correct or help them out, make sure it's done respectfully. Too many elders demand respect but refuse to give it first.

Don't Be Afraid To Compliment Each Other

There's those who love to see others win and succeed, then there's others who hate to see anyone who looks like them doing better than their present circumstances. We have to be people who enjoys to see anyone who looks like us win, regardless if you know this person or not. It's okay to be happy for a complete stranger's success. Always know that whenever you see someone who looks like you or from your circumstances succeed, it means you can succeed as well.

The energy we put out towards others has a way of coming back to us, so treat people as you would like to be treated in your moment of glory. We always have to remember theirs always more to someone's story than we know about. If a person's success was just plain luck that fell out of the sky maybe you won't be as enthusiastic about their success as a person who worked and earned it.

If you knew a person woke up early at 5am everyday to work on their craft before going to work and/or worked hard after their job into the later night or had to overcome difficult odds like homelessness to meet their goals to become successful, not only would you most likely respect this person's success you may even cheer them on and root for them.

The very person some Black people are "hating on" possibly had to overcome obstacles that we would have no choice but to respect. The problem is we do not see everyone's journey to success, so we don't know how they got there. To assume someone is an "over night success" is rooted in jealousy because such a thing does not exist.

One thing to also remember is getting "there" (to success) doesn't really matter because the real work begins when are trying to maintain and grow success. Make sure you are not too judgmental of those who are down on their luck or are in a state of poverty.

A person may be on the brink of success, and you may have been around them just before they are going to have a breakout moment of success. Many of the people we hold with esteem and respect today have had to overcome homelessness, poverty, and misfortune. Regardless of one's current standing in life, it's imperative that we see and celebrate the goodness that each of us has regardless of economic and social class.

Support The Black Community:

We must not only see the value in each other from an individual standpoint, but also from a collective standpoint as well. We cannot want better for the community if we do not believe it is possible. We have to be willing to support Black business, brands, art, music, and programs geared towards the advancement of our people. Our goal should be to shop Black first, after that then the next best available option.

Wanting to see the community as a whole succeed will help one change from a hater mindset into an encouraging mindset. People who hate others live in a world of limitation. They think there's not enough to go around for everybody, so they hate to see others succeed. These people may feel like only a select few can be successful. Make sure you view life with an abundance mindset and not a limited mindset. An abundance mindset will have you thinking theirs enough to go around for everyone.

When we love each other, we can create not just a loving community but also loving neighborhoods. Author-activist **Claude Anderson** once said in an interview it's called the "hood" because it is incomplete. When Black people get back to treating each other neighborly we can work towards living in "neighborhoods" and not the "hood."

We have to be willing to invest, do business, and provide some sort of beneficial service for Black neighborhoods. Even though some of our areas of living are complete eye sores, we should be willing to build them up with pride because what most important is its ours and we love what's ours!

- Have a mindset where you are willing to help others, especially those within your community.

- Rejoice and celebrate all Black success (whether you know the successful person or not).

- Never be jealous or envious of someone else's success. Remember someone's success does not take away from your success and it does not mean you are a failure in comparison.

- Be helpful to other members in your community. Don't be afraid to help strangers, just make sure you are in a safe setting and most of all make sure you ask them if you can help.

- Be helpful but make sure you don't overextend yourself. You can't help others if you are compromised.

- Don't be afraid to compliment others.

- Always have a vision of the Black community being successful. No matter what the community may face, always have the vision and idea that Black people will succeed in whatever endeavors we pursue.

WE WILL BE
SOLUTION
ORIENTED PEOPLE

For many, the perception of Black history starts with slavery in America and having to overcome overwhelming odds just to have equal rights. Many Black people may have a low perception of themselves or their own people because of this.

Theirs a population of Black people in America who feel that the race is doomed to face oppression and will have to be satisfied with whatever is left over, or whatever is allowed for us to do or aspire to be. Too many think with the mindset that Black people collectively will fail in endeavors because of a lack of faith in the people. Some believe even if something successful is accomplished, it will somehow be stolen from us or dismantled in some form or fashion. Some of us see failure no matter what because of community and self-perception.

Theirs no doubt some fears that some Black people have are valid such as a lack of resources that are readily available to other communities. No doubt that in some cases Black people are also responsible for some of the setbacks and in some cases the community. We may have to change some of the traditions normally held in order to be more successful in the future.

Yet and still despite the truthfulness in some of these setbacks, Black people still must have a vision and a belief that we can achieve. Theirs too many examples of Black people overcoming harder circumstances than we face today. Too many of our ancestors before us have made incredible sacrifices and risk during times harder than we could imagine, so we can have the life we live today. We owe it to them to shoot after our goals with 100% belief.

Non-Objectively Looking at the Good and Bad of Black History

Studying the history of your people and country of residence is important because it gives you keys of what to focus on in the future. Study history and see where Black people failed and see where Black people progressed and why. It also doesn't hurt to see what business effective community practices that other cultures and communities.

Some Black people in the recent past have lived a successful life but they aren't as famous as civil rights leaders, or moguls. Do not only learn from the past of famous leaders and situations also study local leaders, and examples in your family of how you should and shouldn't live your life going forward. Looking at the past can help give you a more defined vision of your future or whatever you want to accomplish.

When you go to therapy, usually a therapist will ask you questions about your past, sometimes going all the way back to childhood. The reason for this is because most people's traits and characteristics can and will be formed from past experiences in life.

Also, a lot of the pain that people deal with are reoccurring thoughts of past events in the mind. To effectively deal with the present and provide a better future you must learn and heal from your past. As a community the same rules apply.

Look At Your Goal and Obstacles as A Game You Plan To Win

Always envision yourself accomplishing your goals no matter your present circumstances are. Do not let times of hardship fool you into not accomplishing your goals and do not let victory make you complacent. Keep having the vision until you accomplish whatever you set out to do.

When you look at whatever obstacle that is in the way of your goals as a problem you may start to overly stress over the issue, think with a negative mindset, and or you may think more of what will go wrong instead of what will go right. When you can look at your obstacles as a steppingstone you will think of how you will benefit and grow from the situation. You may look at the situation as a learning lesson instead of a curse. If you are successful in overcoming the obstacle you will have more confidence and vigor going forward.

The author **Dennis Kimbro** wrote a phenomenal book that every Black person should have called, *"Daily Motivation for African-American Success."* The book has stories of African- American success, affirmations, and lessons. I read it every day as it has a passage for everyday of the year. I unfortunately don't remember the page and the story in its entirety, however what I do remember from the story was the man said, "everything in my life happens for my benefit." He was stating that both good and bad things that happens to him are for his benefit. Thinking this way allowed him to navigate through life with less worry and stress because he believed that even bad situations work towards his goals. It's hard to look at situations as losses when you feel that you can benefit from it.

Another book by **Dennis Kimbro** and **Napoleon Hill**, *"Think and Grow Rich A Black Choice"*, had a passage you should keep in mind. Remember this quote when facing tough times in the pursuit of greatness:

"The great illusion called misfortune, when view "rightly" is just-an illusion. Misfortune and set backs are often illusions because we fail to connect the long-term benefits to the negative occurrence.

Whenever you are faced with a knotty dilemma, you always have a clear choice in how you will deal with it. If you brood over the disappointment, you simply magnify your problems out of proportion. It's like taking a pebble off the beach and holding it close to your eyes. This small stone, when held close, can completely black your view. But if you hold it at a proper viewing distance, it can be examined and properly dealt with. If you drop it at your feet, it becomes a stepping stone."

Waiting For the Worst-Case Scenario

One issue with the Black community is we as a collective (not all, but a good majority) wait until the worst-case scenario to take important aspects of living seriously. Many things that are important to our livelihood get put on the back burner in preference of making money and fulfilling wants. In the **"Miseducation of the Negro" Carter G. Woodson** stated the following almost half a century ago about the mindset of many Black people of that time:

"Unless they happen to become naked they never think of the production of cotton or wool; unless they get hungry they never give any thought to the output of wheat and corn; unless their friends lose their jobs they never inquire

288

*about the outlook of coal and steel, or how
these things affect the children they are trying
to teach. In other words, they live in a world,
but are not of it."*

Part of being solution oriented is not expecting
the worst-case scenario, but preparing for it like the
saying goes; *"expect the best but prepare for the
worst"*. Black people in a world that oppresses them
should be prepared to face multiple problems. For
example, this means eating healthy, not waiting
until you have a health problem to do so.

This means arming yourself to protect you and
your family, not waiting until after you have been
robbed or burglarized. This means creating your
own income, not waiting until you get fed up on the
job or fired. We don't know what will happen in this
world so we must be prepared to solve our own
issues. One of the biggest parts of being self-reliant
is being able to depend on yourself in times of
emergency.

Do Black people deserve more from their
governments around the world? Yes! Do Black
people deserve reparations, and better treatment? Of
course! We deserve more no question, but will we
get the things we deserve? Asking and waiting may
not be the best solution for our community. It's not
fair that we must work through problems we did not
create. We deserve more, but we have to be willing
to work, act, and move, as if we will not get what
we deserve from others. We, the Black community,
must always be willing to go after the things we
want, and not wait on others.

- Develop a mindset where you see victory and winning for yourself and your people. Have a vision of what success looks like to you.

- Study this history of Black people where you live and understand how past events have shaped the quality of life.

- After studying the past, find what problems or issues the community has.

- If you have NOT found your purpose in life, build a business that addresses a problem in the Black community.

- Look at every setback as a part of your growth and development. Think with the mindset *"everything that happens to me is for my benefit."*

- Address the problems that you and your people have as soon as possible. Remember if you are in a situation where you need something, but you don't have it, it's already too late. It's better to have it and not need it, than to need it and NOT have it.

- No matter how bad things were and presently are for Black people, always think in terms of the community being successful in the future. What you believe is everything! Hold on to the idea of victory no matter what.

WE WILL BE HAPPY

All the atrocities Black people have faced historically and the ones we face today can cause one to be depressed, feel hopeless, or have bad self-esteem. Throughout it all you have to find a way to be happy in this world! Be sure to understand your history in totality and do not be afraid to be aware of what is negatively affecting Black people. While understanding what the community is against, somehow a Black person must find happiness in it all. If you do not, then the oppressors of Black people will be victorious.

Just because you experience joy in your life does not mean you cannot be passionate about overcoming oppression or lack vigor in your endeavors. Black people having fun and enjoying life despite oppression is a symbolic fight against such because we choose to be happy although we have every reason to be angry. When we choose to be happy, we gain power from our own thoughts, feelings, and emotions instead of being controlled by an exterior force.

Happiness Vs Blissful Ignorance

Some Black people don't need help in this department, in fact some Black people may have too much fun, as in that's all they are worried about. There's a population in the community who are concerned with partying, drug abuse, and obsessive spending, so much that they either choose not to live life more productively or they are ignorant to important issues in favor of keeping the party going. Some of these people use this way of life to mask individual issues or broad issues that a community must deal with.

Being happy and blissfully ignorant is two different things. Being unaware of what's going on with you and your people can be dangerous, as bad things could be happening to you and/or your people that you are unaware of. One issue that many prominent Black people face is once they become successful and life becomes easier, they can get so comfortable that they either forget about the oppression facing them, or they feel like it doesn't exist because of their success. Some unfortunately know full well of the oppression other Black people are facing but are not concerned about it because its not *their* problem or it doesn't affect the people they personally know.

Choosing to be happy despite all the knowledge you have is one of the most powerful things you can do. To combat Black issues and choosing to be happy takes strength, courage, good self-esteem, and self-love. Most of all it shows that you have love for yourself and others.

Just because Black people were born into these circumstance does not mean we have dwell on negative parts of our existence all the time. Yet we also should not aspire to be ignorant of or ignore the issues facing us individually and as a community.

Do not use happiness as a numbing agent to hide or run from responsibilities. Instead weaponize happiness and use it to spread joy to the people you love and come in to contact with. Happiness is a show of faith that your life will work out in your favor no matter what your current circumstances are. True happiness is the belief that better days are coming.

Words of Self Affirmation

In this world you will hear many negative things about you and your people. You will hear negative remakes on TV, the media, your place of work and for some negativity can come from your own family members. Words can be very powerful and even for the strongest of us some words can penetrate the barriers we put up. **Don Miguel Ruiz** stated it perfectly in his book *"The Four Agreements"* he has a chapter called *"Be Impeccable with Your Word"* he says the following:

> *"The word is a powerful tool you have as a human; it is the tool of magic. But like a sword with two edges, your word can create the most beautiful dream or your word can destroy everything around you."*

Where do you get your positive words of affirmation from?

Some people get positive words of encouragement from their family, friends, and co-workers. However, what do you do when you don't get positive feedback from anyone? You cannot guarantee that others will speak encouraging words about you, so make sure you tell yourself what you need to hear. Look yourself in the mirror when you wake up and before you go to sleep and tell yourself "I love you", "I am happy", "I believe in you", and/or "I have what it takes to accomplish what I want." You can come up with your own positive affirmations that are unique to you.

Tell yourself you are worthwhile and that you can and will accomplish what you want. Words are powerful and the words you speak on a consistent basis become your reality. Some Black people have a negative outlook on life because negativity is all they hear. Make sure that you hear positive words about you even if it only comes from *you*.

Finding What Makes You Happy

Happiness is available to everyone, it's just that some choose to find it and embrace it, and some don't. No matter how bad your circumstances are or what you've been through in the past, everyone has something to be happy about. At the very least be happy to be alive. Even if circumstances in your current life may not be what you want them to be, the fact that you are alive means you get another chance to change your life in whatever ways you see fit.

Showing up is half the battle sometimes, and in some cases just trying repeatedly can be enough to get the things you want. You may be surprised what you get out of life when you are persistent. Waking up each day is not only just showing up for life, but you get another chance to live on your terms.

Sometimes we forget that being able to walk is a blessing, being able to see is a blessing, having a means of income is a blessing. Find happiness wherever you can find it. Become aware of what puts you in a better mood. Make sure you can find happiness without the use of external forces. Your happiness needs to come from within instead of relying on external forces like drugs, addictions, and the approval of others.

Asking Black people to be happy while dealing with racism and oppression in this world can be asking a lot, however Black people must find happiness. Choosing to be happy is one of the greatest forms of self-love, and Black people must love themselves first before they can properly love other Black people.

Find something that brings out joy in you. This could be a hobby or an area of interest. You beat oppression when you can be wise to your people's needs all while maintaining peace and happiness. If you are an adult and have lost touch of what makes you happy, think about what you liked to do or your interest you had when you were a child. In young childhood your interests were more intuitive and pure rather than influence from the outside world.

Happiness Can Give You Strength

In my past I would resort to anger often. It wasn't because I felt defeated or had low self worth, in fact it was the opposite. Sometimes I would take on anger to gain passion, drive, and persistence. The reason for this is because I associated anger with power. While some would get angry because they felt like all hope was lost, I was different. When I got angry it was the beginning, not the end. A reason why I embraced anger so much not too long ago, was because I had a negative outlook on my life at that current time.

During this time, I had taken the leap of faith, but I was way in over my head; I was broke, had very little clientele, and had only one check from the job I quit as a means to support myself. Not to mention at that time I was staying in an extended stay where I was paying $150 a week for rent. $150 a week may not seem like a lot to pay, but when you do not have guaranteed work and you are pretty much "winging it" that meager sum to many put a lot of pressure on my shoulders.

Deep down inside I never felt like a loser despite my circumstances. I always felt like a winner inside, but I could not deny the reality of where I was at that time. Since how I felt about myself did not match my reality it caused anger. The opinions of others did not help things either. Many people during this time looked down on me and thought less of me because of my results at the current moment. As you can imagine this just added fuel to the raging fire that was my anger.

I became furious and used that anger to motivate myself out of a dark place. Using anger as motivation worked for me, after all I felt so poor at the time, it made me feel like anger was all I had to depend on. Ironically it worked in my favor!

Being motivated by anger I was able to accomplish great things and took myself to new levels. I accomplished things faster than I thought I would. A year later the poverty was gone and even though I had accomplished more than I set out to, the anger was still there. After a while I realized that it was never my circumstances that ushered in the feelings of anger, I allowed and embraced such a feeling within myself.

I could have easily been motivated by happiness in those same circumstances. Even though my reality then had me looking like a loser, I still had many things to be happy about. I was in a time and place as a person where I was waiting for my external world to make me happy. I wanted so much more out of life. Nothing's wrong with ambition but, you have to be careful not to get to a point where you ignore or belittle the blessings you already have.

Even though I was broke at that time, I was in good health, I could walk, I had somewhere to live, something to eat, and some people did have love for me during that time. Looking back, I had plenty to be happy about. I just ignored it because I wanted so much more it caused me to overlook what I had. I deprived myself of happiness. Now that I'm older and wiser I know that happiness always has and will come from within

Instead of being angry because I was broke, I could have been happy to be able to pursue my passion. Instead of being angry about what outsiders said about me, I could have been happy about how I feel about myself. My mother, my family, my craft, my health, my happiness are all things I could have used as motivation.

Anger is like a fire that you light inside yourself. Good things can happen with fire; you can use it to cook a meal, heat a home, and many things can be created with fire. Even though great things can come from fire you have to put it out or it will continue to burn everything around it. Anger is the same way. You can use it as motivation but at some point, you have to *put it out* or it will damage you mentally and physically. Remember that constant stress on the body and mind will cause both to deteriorate.

You can use happiness as motivation to achieve goals and you will feel great about doing it when the residual affects of happiness is left over. You can use anger as motivation, but it should only be temporary motivation. Just like when you cook a meal, you only need the flame on when you are cooking, once you are done you need to turn the flame off or you could risk burning the entire house down. Use happiness to achieve your goals as a healthier form of motivation.

Happiness & Health

When you are stressed, your body is in fight-or-flight mode. Your brain responds to stress as if you are being attacked by an animal or another human from our primal days of existence. This means we can tend to overly stress on something that is happening in our lives. The problem is when our body is in stress mode, we put our body in conditions to fight to the death or run for your life over things that are important but not worthy of such a response. Being behind on your bills is stressful but it's not a life-or-death situation usually. This is why you can't react to every stressful situation the same. You must put it in perspective, so you don't over stress your body.

When your body is in fight-or-flight mode, blood is driven from the stomach to the muscles slowing down the digestive system. Your metabolism slows and you may have a craving for sweets. You may indulge in "emotional eating" which usually consists of unhealthy foods. All these factors can lead to weight gain if you are dealing with prolonged stress.

The brain is greatly affected in a negative way from prolonged stress. Things like depression, anxiety, and migraines are some of the issues stress brings. More serious conditions include stroke and brain aneurysms.

Your blood pressure will rise and over time can lead to things like a heart attack. Fight-or-flight is not a bad thing. It prepares us to deal with danger. The thing is fight-or-flight is supposed to be a response to a short-term moment, not days to years on end. Prolonged stress makes the body overstimulated in areas like the brain and heart and under stimulated in areas like the stomach. All of which can cause an array of diseases and make any ailment you are dealing with worse.

This is why you must have healthy alternatives for dealing with stress. To ask you not to get mad or stressed out about anything is unrealistic. Even at your best effort, you will get mad at something. How you deal with stress is most important. Meditation, exercise, and watching something funny are all good ways to relieve stress. Activities you like to do are also stress relievers.

Do not use drugs as an alternative to stress. Drugs can lead to negative effects on your health, can have a negative impact on your finances, and can cause even more stress if your drug of choice is not available to you when you want it. Relieve stress and be happy for yourself because it's good for your health. In this life you must do what benefits you, and being happy is very beneficial. You should also benefit others and happiness will equip you to do so.

Happiness & Opportunity

As an entrepreneur, I've found that being in a state of happiness attracts more business to you. Think of it like this, would you rather approach a happy person or an angry person? Most people would rather approach a happy person because a happy person is usually more inviting. When someone is angry, they can give off the energy and appearance that they don't want anyone to bother them. If people can't approach you, they won't spend their money with you.

If someone is approached by a person who appears to be angry, they may have their guard up. If they are approached by a person who is happy it may bring their guard down. Happy energy brings and invites more people in. When you can attract more people, you will get more sales and more opportunities.

Sometimes I do a good job at relieving stress and sometimes I don't. The times that I don't, I refuse to let what I'm going through get in the way of business. If I'm stressed about something I can put it away and not think about it when working. Nothing is worse than trying to do business with someone who has an attitude about something else.

Your brain is like a magnet. It will attract what you keep it focused on. Stay angry and stressed and more of which will come in your life. Stay happy and positive and more of such is in store. Being happy is a form of faith that all will be well in your life. Never lose that faith, and always find a reason to be happy.

- Despite where you are in life, find happiness in some way or form.

- Understand that happiness comes from within. Do NOT rely on external forces alone to make you happy like; drugs, material things, or the opinions of others.

- Do NOT mistake happiness for blissful ignorance. There is power in knowledge and it should not be disregarded for happiness. Find a balance where you can be well informed and still know happiness and peace.

- Make it a daily routine to say positive words of affirmations to yourself. You may not hear positive opinions about yourself from others, make sure you are at least hearing positive words from yourself.

- Make it a habit to compliment yourself. The goal here is to build confidence and happiness, not arrogance and vanity.

- Life will throw many responsibilities at you. Make time in your life for the things that make you happy. Have a hobby that you engage in that brings you joy and passion.

- Try not to be motivated by anger. If you choose such a motivator, make sure its temporary for if held on for too long can cause mental and physical damage to your health.

- Be motivated by happiness. Being happy is a strong emotion and can be used to do great things. One can be motivated and do great things being happy just as they could embracing anger. You would rather have the residual effects of happiness than anger.

- Remember happiness is good for your health and stress is bad for your health.

- Happiness is faith, never lose faith and be happy!

Conclusion

Theirs no doubt that Black people worldwide have a difficult task in front of them. To live their everyday lives while dealing with racism and systematic oppression. The good news is we do not have to combat such issues alone, we can be together in this fight. We can rely on each other and lean on each other in our times of need. We do not have to be in competition with each other, we can instead help each other. We can go places that we could never reach as individuals.

I hope the passages in this book reached you and if you had a negative outlook on Black people, I hope this has change your way of thinking. If you already had knowledge of self, confidence, and love for Black people, my hope is that this book helped reinforced your positive thoughts of the race.

The collection of Black people worldwide should be proud of the accomplishments that have been made despite racism and oppression. We cannot just be satisfied for what we have at this current moment alone. We all owe it to the ancestors who endured before us and the generations after us to strive for more greatness. The youth are depending on us to better ourselves and the world around us as much as possible so they can have better opportunities than we have now.

As for Black people we truly do not know how many allies outside of our race will love us and fight for us. We may have some, but we cannot guarantee allies, we must guarantee we will have our own backs. My hope is that more align with us than against us but that is up to them and how they see us, which will always be their choice. Black people have a choice too. We can be separate individuals, or we can be people who will always have each other's backs even if we don't know each other personally.

More volumes of this book will be made soon to serve the interest of Black people. More problems and issues that negatively affect Black people will be addressed in the future and ideas/concepts that benefit Black people will be highlighted and celebrated. Simply put the goal of this book is bring Black people together to preserve a better future for us all.

To Black people worldwide, this book was made because I love you, I want to see you all happy, healthy, and successful. I want you, the reader, to have love for all people, however given Black oppression and racism worldwide, I want you especially love yourself and to love the people who look like you.

References:

The Power of Your Subconscious Mind by Joseph Murphy 148, 1963.

Think And Grow Rich A Black Choice, by Dennis Kimbro & Napoleon Hill 56, 54. 1991.

The Miseducation of the Negro by Carter G. Woodson. 27, 56, 48, 49, 55. 1933.

Powernmoics by Dr. Claude Anderson. 20, 81. 2000.

The Four Agreements by Don Miguel. Ruiz. 260. 1997.

The 21 Irrefutable Laws of Leadership by John C. Maxwell. 22. 1998.

Rich Dad Poor Dad by Robert Kiyosaki. 126, 147. 2012.

Black Power Inc. The New Voice of Success by Cora Daniels. 91, 130, 143. 2004.

7 Steps to Discover Your Inner Greatness by Cyrus Ausar. 19. 2019.

Black Fatherhood: The Guide to Male Parenting by Earl Hutchinson. 12, 104, 106. 1995.

Dr. Claude Anderson: Ugly truths about reparation, affirmative action (6:54).

48 Laws of Power by Robert Greene. 22, 56. 1998.

Daily Motivations for African American Success by Dennis Kimbro. 249. 1993.

Black Privilege: Opportunity Comes to Those Who Create It by Charlamagne Tha God 34. 2017.

Visit our website to stay up to date with books, comics, and Eye Gift Publishing news:

WWW.EYEGIFTPUBLISHING.COM

www.ingramcontent.com/pod-product-compliance
Lightning Source LLC
Chambersburg PA
CBHW052122270326
41930CB00012B/2717